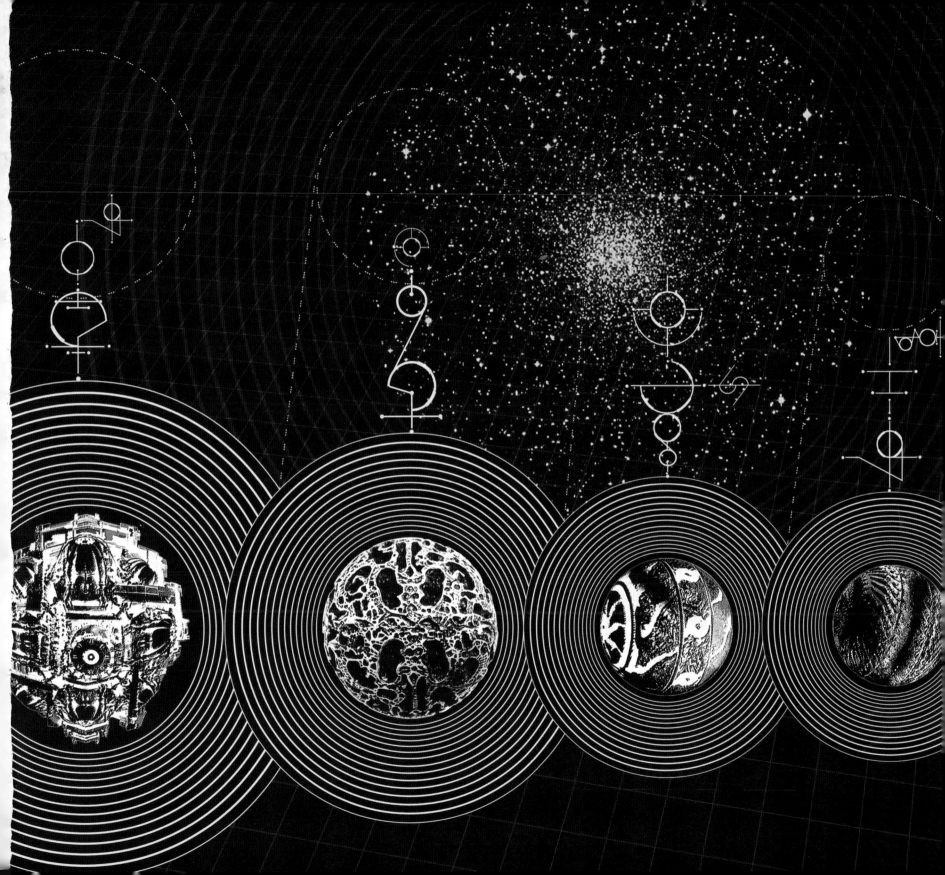

Limited-edition collectible poster by Charlie Wen. San Diego Comic-Con 2013.

MARVEL STUDIOS
THE INFINITY SAGA

THE ART OF
MARVEL STUDIOS
GUARDIANS OF THE GALAXY

WRITTEN BY
MARIE JAVINS

BOOK DESIGN BY
JEFF POWELL

FOREWORD BY
JAMES GUNN

AFTERWORD BY
CHARLIE WEN

DUSTJACKET ART BY
CHARLIE WEN

TITAN BOOKS

FOR MARVEL PUBLISHING
JEFF YOUNGQUIST, Editor
SARAH SINGER, Editor,
 Special Projects
JEREMY WEST, Manager,
 Licensed Publishing
SVEN LARSEN, VP, Licensed
 Publishing
DAVID GABRIEL, SVP Print,
 Sales & Marketing
C.B. CEBULSKI, Editor in Chief

FOR MARVEL STUDIOS 2014
KEVIN FEIGE, President
LOUIS D'ESPOSITO, Co-President
VICTORIA ALONSO, Executive
 Vice President, Visual Effects
JEREMY LATCHAM, Senior
 Vice President, Production &
 Development
JONATHAN SCHWARTZ,
 Vice President, Production
 & Development
WILL CORONA PILGRIM, Creative
 Manager, Research & Development
RYAN POTTER, Principal Counsel
ERIKA DENTON, Clearances Manager
RANDY McGOWAN, VP Technical
 Operations
ELENI ROUSSOSS, Digital Asset
 Coordinator
DAVID GRANT, Vice President,
 Physical Production
ALEXIS AUDITORE, Physical Assets
 Coordinator

MARVEL STUDIOS' THE INFINITY SAGA –
GUARDIANS OF THE GALAXY:
THE ART OF THE MOVIE

ISBN: 9781803365626
E-BOOK ISBN: 9781803367408

First edition: December 2024

10 9 8 7 6 5 4 3 2 1

Published by Titan Books
A division of Titan Publishing Group Ltd
144 Southwark St, London SE1 0UP

www.titanbooks.com

© 2024 MARVEL

No similarity between any of the names, characters, persons, and/or institutions in this book with those of any living or dead person or institution is intended, and any such similarity that may exist is purely coincidental.

Did you enjoy this book? We love to hear from our readers. Please e-mail us at: readerfeedback@titanemail.com or write to Reader Feedback at the above address.

To receive advance information, news, competitions, and exclusive offers online, please sign up for the Titan newsletter on our website: www.titanbooks.com

No part of this publication may be reproduced, stored in a retrieval system, or transmitted, in any form or by any means without the prior written permission of the publisher, nor be otherwise circulated in any form of binding or cover other than that in which it is published and without a similar condition being imposed on the subsequent purchaser.

A CIP catalogue record for this title is available from the British Library.

Printed in China

Andy Park keyframe.

Charlie Wen concept art.

CONTENTS

9 FOREWORD
BY JAMES GUNN

10 INTRODUCTION
A THIEF, TWO THUGS,
AN ASSASSIN, AND A MANIAC

16 CHAPTER ONE
THE LEGENDARY STAR-LORD

70 CHAPTER TWO
DARK ALLIANCES

108 CHAPTER THREE
GALAXY'S MOST WANTED

148 CHAPTER FOUR
CORPS VALUES

174 CHAPTER FIVE
PRISON BREAK

230 CHAPTER SIX
KNOWHERE TO RUN

274 CHAPTER SEVEN
FAMILY REUNION

296 CHAPTER EIGHT
SOMEBODY'S GOTTA DO IT

320 CHAPTER NINE
MARKETING GUARDIANS
OF THE GALAXY

326 AFTERWORD
BY BILL BRZESKI

328 CONTRIBUTOR BIOS

332 ACKNOWLEDGMENTS

335 ARTIST CREDITS

Chris Foss concept art.

FOREWORD

Exactly two years ago Marvel called me in to discuss directing *Guardians of the Galaxy*. I must admit—at first I wasn't sold. I love Marvel comics and I love Marvel movies and I even love raccoons (I had a raccoon figurine collection as a child). But I don't do a film unless it's in my bones. For me to spend years of my life directing a film and sacrificing all other endeavors, it needs to feel like a calling, and I need to feel like I'm bringing something specific to the film that wouldn't be brought by another director. And as Co-Producers Jeremy Latcham and Jonathan Schwartz sat there trying to tell me why *Guardians of the Galaxy* was such a great idea for a film, and why I was so good for it, I didn't fully see it. No lightning bolt hit me. No visions of God's finger poking down from the heavens prodding me forward.

And, in truth, the whole idea seemed a little weird. Yes, I knew who the *Guardians of the Galaxy* were, and thought they were cool, but I'm a comic-book geek. The rest of the world thinks Gamora is someone who fights Godzilla. And the general audience might like a talking raccoon if he was chasing a nut in a Pixar film, but brandishing a machine gun? It was pretty apparent to me Marvel had lost their minds.

So I nodded and smiled at Jeremy and Jonathan. I said "Cool" a lot. They showed me some early artwork, which was pretty, but not enough to persuade me, and I nodded and smiled some more. And then I shook their hands and left. I promised to think about *Guardians*, but I was sure I was going to get home and call my agent and have him tell Marvel I wasn't interested. I knew I wasn't the first director they had approached. And those others had probably declined for the same reasons I was about to—the concept was just too fricking out there for a gigantic, big budget spectacle.

I got into my car to start the hour-long drive from Manhattan Beach, where Marvel was located at the time, to my home in Studio City. And as I was pulling onto the 405, it happened. The lightning bolt hit me, the finger of God came down from the sky and grazed my skull, and I saw it completely. *Guardians of the Galaxy* was the movie I had been waiting my whole life to do.

At first it was mostly a visual thing. At that point I wasn't talking to Marvel about rewriting the script, as I went on later to do, but just directing. I have loved science fiction my whole life. To be more specific, I have loved space epics, or space operas, or space adventures, as long as I can remember. And this was the chance to make one for today's audience, a relevant film that cherished the films I loved from the past, while not repeating them.

Alien and *Blade Runner* are groundbreaking films, but so many science fiction films have been entombed by them, relying on darkness and grittiness to make them "real." The look of science fiction films has mostly been hitting the same piano key over and over since that time. And if they aren't *Blade Runner*, they're the descendants of *Logan's Run*, where the future and alternate realities are composed of almost all white buildings, and entire planets seem to have all of their buildings designed by a single architect.

Guardians of the Galaxy would be about color, and life. In-your-face, over-the-top, unrepentant COLOR. We would rescue the aesthetics of pulpy science fiction films from the fifties and sixties—films like *Forbidden Planet*, *Fantastic Voyage*, *Barbarella*—while simultaneously retaining the grittiness and workaday reality of later films.

Our palette would be explicitly post-modern with contrasting colors and architecture and items. We'd see old buildings next to new ones. We'd see futuristic technology as the backdrop for the retro Sony Walkman. We'd see barren, dead landscapes with beautiful, nebulous skies overhead (for this I'd show everyone who came on board Magritte's *Empire of Light* series of paintings, to which I am deeply indebted). We would take glorious advantage of shooting in 3-D, something rare for movies these days. We would not be bashful.

And the raccoon, the raccoon that initially seemed to be such a hurdle — the raccoon was the best part. The raccoon wouldn't be Bugs Bunny in the middle of the *Avengers*. Sure, at a distance the raccoon might look cute—like when you dress up your dog for Halloween. But when you would get up close you would see into his dark, animal eyes, and he would be hauntingly real. This was not a life he had asked for. He was an animal, a simple beast, torn apart and put back together in a series of horrifying experiments, and now he was completely, and utterly, alone. We would completely deconstruct and build back up the anthropomorphic animal. I have never been a raccoon and I have never been torn apart and put back together, but in that car ride home I fell in love with Rocket like I had rarely fallen in love with anyone. From that moment on, he became like a son to me. Or, perhaps more accurately, my id.

My synapses fired like crazy for that hour-long ride. Once home, I immediately sat down at my computer and typed up a fifteen-page document on how I would visually direct *Guardians of the Galaxy*, and I went from mild disinterest to real, true need. I needed to make this movie. And, as self important as this may or may not sound, I felt like it needed me.

As should be apparent by now, I got the gig. There was only one problem. All of that stuff I just talked about? I couldn't do any of it. I mean, I can draw, a little. But I can't design spaceships, or buildings, or worlds. My character designs are only slightly more complex than emojis. And every time I've tried to light one of my own films, I'd set something on fire.

So in the wake of my amateur visions came a team of professionals who helped to bring them to life—not in the way I imagined, but better.

First are my Marvel teammates—Producer Kevin Feige; Executive Producers Louis D'Esposito, Victoria Alonso, and the aforementioned Jeremy Latcham; and Co-Producer Jonathan Schwartz. We shared a vision from its inception. They collaborated without ego—something exceedingly rare in Hollywood. They supported my strengths and watched my back when my weaknesses occurred or when we faced other obstacles. They have been the best artistic partners I've ever had.

Our vision was furthered by Charlie Wen, the head of visual development on *Guardians of the Galaxy*. Charlie and his team churned out thousands of works of art—most of them worthy of hanging in an art gallery. They also helped to design many of the characters and outfits and objects throughout the film.

Then there was Charlie Wood, our production designer. Charlie and I spent countless hours in my dining room drawing doodles on paper scraps and talking about how various alien cultures could influence their environments. We took inspiration from everywhere—muscle cars, World War II aircraft, the movie *The Right Stuff*, and the artwork of '70s and '80s science fiction illustrator Chris Foss (Chris's work was a part of my original pitch to Marvel—so it was fitting that Charlie pulled him out of retirement and hired him to help us design spaceships). Charlie and I would talk about all of this stuff endlessly—most of it just for our own benefit but, thankfully, some of it for yours. Charlie's production team designed most of the spaceships and the majority of the sets and worlds we visit in *Guardians*.

Alexandra Byrne, our costume designer, was a dream. Her attention to detail is without par. If you've seen the movie, please watch it again, and notice how amazing all of the clothing is up close. They are as unique in the micro as they are in the macro, lived in, practical, specific, and glorious.

David White was the special make-up effects designer—he created many of the characters in the film and almost all of the background aliens, and he also brought Charlie Wen's creatures seamlessly to life. His job was as daunting as anyone's—along with Elizabeth Yianni-Georgiou, our head of make-up, he'd sometimes have to turn over a hundred Londoners into aliens in a single day.

Then there was the amazing Stephane Ceretti, our visual effects supervisor, and the lunatics over at Framestore and MPC, the visual effects companies responsible for bringing the final looks of Rocket and Groot to life, the folks who loved these two beings as much as I did, and who would regularly move me to tears (as well as my assistant, Simon Hatt, who would cry at the drop of a his last name).

My storyboard artists, David Krentz, Bryan and Daniel Andrews, Jane Wu, and others, were able to take my tiny storyboard sketches which looked at best like Fisher-Price people and at worst like a three-year-old's scribbles and transform them into something dynamic and understandable by the entire crew, adding new elements along the way.

And finally, there was Ben Davis, the director of photography. He was the one who was able to take all of these insane ideas and bring them to life with shadow and light.

And of course there are hundreds more. Many whose names I know and just don't have enough room here, and others whose names I don't know—I am utterly grateful for each and every one of them. They all put their hearts and souls into this story of ours.

This book contains work that once belonged to them and now belongs to you. I hope it inspires you to dream, and create, and love. Or, to use the language we now all share, I am Groot.

James Gunn
Sunday, June 1, 2014

INTRODUCTION
A THIEF, TWO THUGS, AN ASSASSIN, AND A MANIAC

Whenever evil threatens the cosmos, 12 billion citizens across the galaxy expect the Nova Corps to keep them safe.

They don't count on putting their lives in the hands of a brash thief, a walking tree, a talking raccoon, a lethal assassin, and a deadly maniac. No one expects much from these underachieving outlaws—least of all, themselves.

All heroes start somewhere.

"The Guardians are all loners or the last of their kind," Executive Producer Jeremy Latcham says. "They meet in jail. They're kind of a mess. You're not sure if they're going to pull it off."

Before the film was announced, few non-fans had heard of *Guardians of the Galaxy*, a relatively obscure comic-book series, and 99 percent of the story takes place on the other side of the universe from the previous films of the Marvel Cinematic Universe. "I think *Guardians of the Galaxy* is the boldest film we've made since the first Iron Man in terms of it being unexpected," Kevin Feige, Producer and President of Marvel Studios says.

A misfit-themed space opera scored with a 1970s soundtrack was not the obvious next step for Marvel Studios after its runaway successes with the core characters of *Marvel's The Avengers*.

"Once you set that bar, where do you go from there?" asks Executive Producer and EVP of VFX and Post-Production Victoria Alonso. "Well, you don't go higher. You take a left turn and you do *Guardians of the Galaxy*."

And yet *Guardians* is very much a Marvel film. It carries the trademark humor and quirkiness audiences have grown to expect from Marvel Studios, along with a unique cast of characters with strong personalities.

"It's the funniest of the Marvel movies," Director and Co-Writer James Gunn says. "I would also say it's the most dramatic of the Marvel movies, and the most emotional."

That emotion comes through five restless misfits—stunted by years of pain, tragedy, and loneliness—who bond together first as a team, then as a family. No raccoon, it seems, is an island.

"Peter Quill lost his mother at a very early age," Co-Producer Jonathan Schwartz explains. "Gamora was raised by villains and her real parents were killed by them, and she was forced to become a weapon. Drax's family was killed by Ronan. Rocket isn't really a raccoon—he's a total misfit and a genetic experiment. Groot is the ultimate outsider and doesn't fit in anywhere. They've all lost their families each in their own way. Necessity has made them each

Cover to *Guardians of the Galaxy* (2008) #1 by Clint Langley.

self-interested—but when they band together, they learn they can actually have family."

The Guardians are not the only ones on screen building their own alliances and bonds. Cosmic super villain Thanos raises both Gamora and Nebula, but he isn't the most stellar father figure. He teaches them ruthlessness and mentors his adopted daughters in the art of dispatching his enemies. He also works with Ronan and Korath, and only Gamora eventually realizes the situation is dysfunctional.

"Gamora made a very active choice as a character to leave and seek out a better life," Latcham explains. "We see a shred of her past relationship with Nebula, but Nebula is so brainwashed and so drawn into this world that she's living in that she just thinks Gamora's gone soft."

Gamora is initially out to get the orb herself so she can sell it to the Collector—an eccentric extraterrestrial whose lab contains artifacts from all over the universe—and make a bit of money to start her new life. She's something good and something bad. But so are the other Guardians.

Alonso sums it up: "Sometimes the oddest of people are your friends. And if you work together, you can make something out of it, regardless of your differences."

The comic-book series that influenced the film was launched in 2008, after a 13-year hiatus since *Guardians of the Galaxy* had last been published in 1995. While the latter series took place in the future, the former existed in the same timeline as the rest of the Marvel Universe.

"The current *Guardians* grew out of an event called *Annihilation*, which was masterminded by Editor Andy Schmidt and Keith Giffen, who wrote it," co-writer Dan Abnett says.

"Andy Schmidt was a huge fan of Marvel's cosmic universe, and pushed to revive it," co-writer Andy Lanning adds.

Schmidt had been a fan of Marvel's cosmic stories since he was a kid, when writer/artist Jim Starlin had helped develop a complex, world-spanning architecture of epic stories revolving around a tremendous power struggle between the hero Captain Marvel and the omnipotent, villainous Thanos.

"The landscape was so vast with various solar systems and empires, and we wanted to bring the stakes back to a galactic conflict," Schmidt says. "But the characters were capable of levity in the face of these situations. So tonally, I wanted to keep that—to make the reader laugh and have fun in the face of all that danger.

"The work we were doing with Marvel's super heroes at the time was down-to-earth and often dark. It was time for some really crazy and colorful heroes to emerge in the Marvel Universe."

After *Annihilation*, Editor Bill Rosemann took over the cosmic universe. Rosemann worked with Giffen and artist Timothy Green

Debrief logs from *Guardians of the Galaxy (2008) #1* and *#3-4*—written by Dan Abnett and Andy Lanning, penciled by Paul Pelletier, inked by Rick Magyar, colored by Nathan Fairbairn and Guru-eFX, and lettered by Virtual Calligraphy's Joe Caramagna.

on the *Annihilation: Conquest—Starlord* miniseries, laying the foundation for the team that would soon became the *Guardians of the Galaxy*.

Rosemann paged through the *Official Handbook of the Marvel Universe* looking for potential members for Star-Lord's *Dirty Dozen*-inspired team, which met in a Kree prison. He took the list to Executive Editor Tom Brevoort, who read it and laughed.

"Tom told me I had picked characters from every decade since the creation of the *Guardians of the Galaxy* in 1969, except I was missing one from the sixties," Rosemann says. "He suggested I pick one, but Marvel didn't have many cosmic characters then, so Tom brought up the old monsters."

Rosemann opened up the *Marvel Monsters* handbook to the entry for Groot, a tree-like extraterrestrial whose 1960 invasion of Earth had been repelled by a scientist using termites.

"Every team needs a big guy," he continues. "Keith Giffen—who had actually created Rocket Raccoon in 1976 with Bill Mantlo—is the one who paired up Rocket and Groot. He said, 'One's a tree and one's a raccoon. I figured they'd be buddies.'"

Green initially drew branches shooting wildly off of Groot in the *Annihilation: Conquest—Starlord* miniseries, then later redesigned the character for the *Annihilators* limited series. "I wanted a much thinner and scarier look," Green says. "I was most excited to draw Rocket Raccoon, though. I'd read that series as a kid. He already looked pretty cool, but I wanted to give him a more petite look. I loved the design for Star-Lord. I wish I could take credit for that, but a very talented artist named Marko Djurdjevic redesigned him."

When Dan Abnett and Andy Lanning began writing the 2008 *Guardians of the Galaxy* series, they built on Giffen's new Star-Lord team. "Dan and I channeled our 12-year-old comic fans. We had the same touchstones of cosmic characters we liked," Lanning says. He and Abnett cherry-picked from the vast number of cosmic characters and environments Marvel had produced through the years. Originally, the relationship to previous incarnations of the team was tenuous.

"We didn't reboot *Guardians of the Galaxy* so much as borrow the name," Abnett says. "The original 1969 *Guardians* lineup by Arnold Drake and Gene Colan was very different, indeed, but we slowly teased the strands together to create an awareness of the previous continuity."

Artist Paul Pelletier joined Abnett and Lanning to launch the 2008 series, building on Green's work and refining character designs over the seven issues he drew. He simplified Star-Lord's mask, and his Rocket was less realistic. "That allowed me to give his face more expression, to really bring out his personality," Pelletier says. "Groot wasn't much more than a sprout during my run, though."

Drax and Gamora joined the team next. "With Drax, it was all about a brooding tough guy with big muscles and tattoos. With Gamora, I wanted to get the point across that she was extremely lethal yet sexy at the same time, green skin and all."

Marvel Studios picked up the core Guardians from the Abnett/Lanning run. But Yondu, Peter Quill's parental figure, came from the original Guardians and the long 1990s run, primarily written and drawn by Jim Valentino. "I added Yondu," says Gunn, who had read the comics as a kid. "He's the one older *Guardians of the Galaxy* member who's a huge part of this movie, although his mythology is mostly different in the film."

Feige believes the cast of characters is the most unique Marvel Studios has ever featured in one of its films. "When we talk about the

Nebula, from 1994 Marvel Masterpieces Card #82 by Greg and Tim Hildebrandt.

The Collector, from *Thanos Quest* (1990) #2—penciled by Ron Lim, inked by John Beatty, and colored by Tom Vincent.

Ronan, from the cover to *Annihilation: Ronan #1* by Gabriele Dell'Otto.

raccoon and the tree, we get a lot of funny looks. And we like funny looks, because funny looks are challenging to us. Funny looks say, 'How are you going to pull that off?' And frankly, if we don't get funny looks at the beginning of a project we're working on, we think we're doing something wrong.

"When you have a group with a human, two alien humanoids and two very alien-looking creatures, you have to find ways to make them relatable," he says. "And in the source material and in the great Marvel comics, they've already done that for us."

Rosemann gives a big nod to those who built and kept alive the Marvel cosmic universe. "We stand on the shoulders of giants," he says. "We owe a debt of gratitude to people like Jim Starlin and Jim Valentino. Without them, there would be no us."

Valentino, meanwhile, cites writer Steve Gerber as his top influence. Gerber had brought back the *Guardians of the Galaxy* in 1974 in *Marvel Two-in-One*, and went on to chronicle their continuing adventures starting in 1976 in *Marvel Premiere*. "I did the best I could to honor and expand upon the personalities he established for the characters. His work still holds up. He really was amazing."

Comics are collaborative, drawing on the work of dozens of creators over several decades. Abnett and Lanning wrote together for 25 years, and they grew up on Starlin and Giffen's work before later working alongside these architects of the cosmos.

A comic-book editor organizes and holds a title's creative team together, keeping track of each character and the production schedule as the collaborative effort proceeds. The filmmaking process is far grander in scale; for *Guardians*, Visual Development Coordinator Jacob Johnston created a document internally nicknamed "The Mother of All Grids" to keep track of the progress, latest iteration, current notes, and due dates for every design element in the film.

"This was the first time we've had to create a world entirely from whole cloth," Latcham notes. "Aside from the two minutes the film takes place in Missouri, the entire thing is out in the universe. Every pair of shoes, every door handle, every hat, every prop—it all had to be created, because we did not want to be in a situation where people said, 'They bought that at the store and they painted it.' When you're trying to avoid that familiarity, you have to constantly look for new things and new ways to do things. Between costumes and props and production design and set dressing, there's just so much innovation happening across the board. Our team had to find new manufacturing processes, to source unexpected products that are real on Earth and define cool ways to alter them so they wouldn't be recognizable. I think the team did an incredible job."

Latcham and Schwartz assembled a presentation file to maintain a consistent visualization of the movie.

"We called it the Matriarch Deck, and we constantly updated it with the latest and greatest art," Schwartz explains. "It helped us present the movie to partners, licensees, and Disney teammates."

The "mother of all decks" included work from Visual Development, which takes the lead on character design; Costume Design; Special Makeup Effects; Production Design, which builds the sets and environments; and Visual Effects tests.

"Concept art is our lifeblood," D'Esposito says. "It inspires characters, scenes, sets, action, set pieces, story lines—and, most importantly, the art inspires us and our filmmakers. We set up what we call our 'War Room,' where the walls are covered with artwork that tells the story of the film from the first scene to the last. Each one of these is our Sanctum Sanctorum. The place where we go to think, be inspired, focus, refocus, and inspire others. The amount of art that is generated for each film is enormous."

Everyone must work in unison to make certain all these pieces add up to a cohesive whole. "The huge amount of collaboration that happened is really unprecedented," Latcham says. "It's a gigantic 24/7 machine that went on for months and months while this world was being designed. It's such a fascinating process."

Costume Designer Alexandra Byrne was also inspired by the production's collaborative nature. "A lot of the images have somebody's name on them, but they're a combination of people from L.A. to London. Everybody brings their own skills, and the design that works is a crossover of ideas and evolution."

Byrne cites Gunn as the source of the collaborative and creative tone. "James was so passionate and ready to answer all questions. It was very easy to get the information. He knew the script and the characters inside out, and he could answer anything and everything that we had questions about."

Finding the right filmmaker for each film is key, and one of they most difficult aspects of the producers' jobs.

"This was a film that was very different than anything we had ever done before," D'Esposito says. "We all knew that tone—the way both the humor and drama were handled

Nova (Richard Rider), from the cover to *Nova (2007) #1* by Adi Granov.

Cover to *Nova (2007) #22* by Juan Doe.

and related to each other—was of utmost importance. We have always been diligent in our searches for filmmakers. Jeremy Latcham and Jonathan Schwartz led the charge and left no stone unturned when it came to the search of the Guardians director."

And Latcham knew Gunn was the right choice from the moment they met.

"He walked in the door, and it became apparent that he'd been genetically engineered in a laboratory somewhere to direct *Guardians of the Galaxy*," Latcham says with a laugh. "He was such a perfect fit. He understood Rocket. He understood Groot. He understood the appeal of those two characters in the middle of this thing. He understood the comedy, the stakes, the need to have real action, but also to have fun. And he came with such a fresh pitch—this idea of the tape of seventies music—which was so unexpected and gives the movie a really grounded feel, while still being totally out of the world.

"From the outset, James had all of the right characteristics and the passion. And he also very much fits the mold of the filmmakers that we like, which is guys who we know have tons of potential and ability but have never been given a canvas this size."

Alonso agrees. "James is an incredibly smart, talented, and funny guy, and a great storyteller. He also has a deep love for raccoons."

Gunn appreciates more than just small, furry mammals. "I'm always attracted to the outcasts and the loners and the losers and the oddballs and the geeks," Gunn says. "That's my culture from which I sprang, so those are my people. And the Guardians are those people, too."

"Each of them are loners, or the last of their kinds," Feige says. "Circumstances force them to come together for the greater good. And through that and the encounters they have with each other, they begin to learn what it means to be a team and to become these *Guardians of the Galaxy*."

Alonso sees Star-Lord, Gamora, Drax, Rocket, and Groot as creating a new family among their peers and common work. "I think we all do that. Some of us are lucky enough to have our families. But those that don't, we find our families in our common fields, whether that's work or hobbies or faith. That's what we do."

Yondu, from *Guardians of the Galaxy Annual (1991) #3*—penciled by Colleen Doran, inked by Steve Montano and colored by Evelyn Stein.

CHAPTER ONE
THE LEGENDARY STAR-LORD

Charming and cunning, overgrown teenager Peter Quill is an incorrigible flirt who ekes out a scavenger's living across the stars. He pilots the Milano, the spaceship equivalent of a souped-up Mustang, and grooves to the beat of a vintage cassette player.

"Peter Quill is a man out of time and also a man out of place," Co-Producer Jonathan Schwartz says. "At a very young age, he was taken from Earth into outer space, and he has to make his own way in this strange universe. Emotionally, Quill is the kid that was left behind, the kid that grew up on Earth in the '80s, and he takes that with him."

Frightened and confused by his mother's death and his father's absence, the young Quill is raised to adulthood by the rough-and-ready aliens who abducted him from Earth. In his search for a valuable Orb, he betrays those closest to him—including his dysfunctional adoptive family.

The idea of a kid from Earth raised among the stars grounds the film. "That was the heart of the story, to have someone that audiences immediately could relate to," Executive Producer Jeremy Latcham says.

And Quill's roots link him to the broader Marvel Cinematic Universe. "He left Earth at a time that Tony Stark would have been a younger man, Bruce Banner would have been a younger man, and Captain America would've been frozen in the ice," Latcham says. "He encounters intergalactic elements we are familiar with from other Marvel films."

Tim Hill keyframe.

STAR-LORD (PETER JASON QUILL)

Peter Quill fancies himself a legendary swashbuckler, adopting the moniker Star-Lord.

"Peter is a traveler, a thief, someone who is as traveled as he is dangerous," says Marvel Studios Head of Visual Development Charlie Wen, who started with Quill's comic-book design and refined his approach as the script evolved. "I began implementing these ideas into his costume. With his long coat, I wanted to introduce a patchwork look—a mismatched, eclectic feel to further sell his accumulation of 'passport travel stamps.'"

Costume Designer Alexandra Byrne oversaw the process of realizing Wen's concepts. "When you work with a concept for a costume on an actor, you're working with their body, their physique, their movement, and with stunts in mind," Byrne says. "If the script dictates they carry a certain weapon, it has to be part of the fitting. Quill's pistol had to be holstered without spoiling or interfering with the lines of the costumes. How he carries his guns should be part of the costume. We worked closely with Props, and we ended up with the whole side of the trouser being designed and constructed so the holster is built into the trouser leg."

Charlie Wen concept art.

CHAPTER ONE: THE LEGENDARY STAR-LORD

"Star-Lord is our main hero, but his traditional look in the comics is anti-hero-like," Concept Artist Andy Park says. "He even could look like a villain if not done correctly. One of the first things I tried was opening up his traditionally closed helmet to reveal his hair. Everyone seemed to respond to that."

Andy Park concept art.

Artist Marko Djurdjevic redesigned Star-Lord for the comics in 2007. "The 'Lord' part of 'Star-Lord' made Marko think of a British Lord," Editor Bill Rosemann explains. "He looked at British soldier uniforms from World War I, and that's where the look comes from. The mask is futurized, but based on a British World War I gas mask."

Kevin Chen concept art.

Andy Park concept art.

CHAPTER ONE: THE LEGENDARY STAR-LORD

"James was adamant about making sure the technology felt Space Age, but not too advanced or over-the-top," Wen says. "It needed to almost feel timeless as in space/time is generally just relative."

Charlie Wen concept art.

CHAPTER ONE: THE LEGENDARY STAR-LORD

Costume FX Supervisor Graham Churchyard worked with the production team to create Star-Lord's realistic, detailed mask. "We had to develop a way that actor Chris Pratt could see and hear clearly while the adjustable red LEDs were fully lit," Churchyard says. "It also needed to be waterproof and to accommodate a remote-control cooling fan, which could be switched off to record dialogue during takes."

Andy Park concept art.

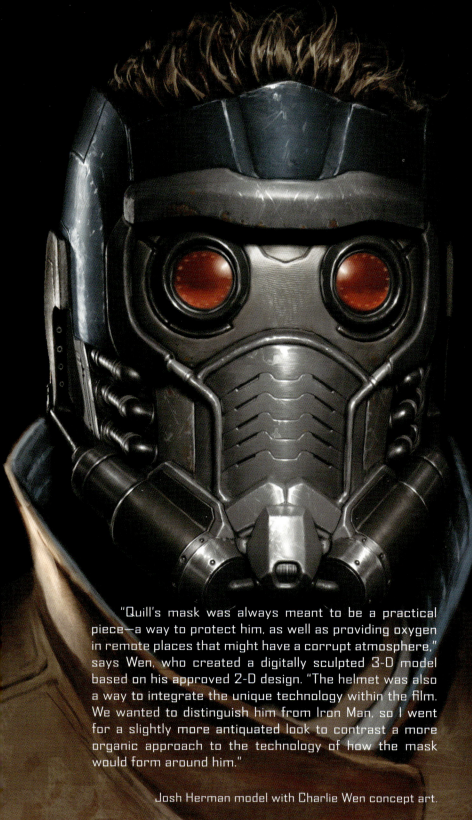

"Quill's mask was always meant to be a practical piece—a way to protect him, as well as providing oxygen in remote places that might have a corrupt atmosphere," says Wen, who created a digitally sculpted 3-D model based on his approved 2-D design. "The helmet was also a way to integrate the unique technology within the film. We wanted to distinguish him from Iron Man, so I went for a slightly more antiquated look to contrast a more organic approach to the technology of how the mask would form around him."

Josh Herman model with Charlie Wen concept art.

Churchyard's team in London took the baton and ran with it. "We sculpted in real clay so that everyone could in Los Angeles look at proportions," Churchyard says. "It's a quick way of looking at different expressions, which was important to the finished look."

The team then used a 3-D printer to create a wearable working prototype based on the finished 3-D model. "After camera-test approval, we then made six hero Star-Lord masks using vacuum casting to capture the fine detail," Churchyard says. "We also added real metal components to compliment the molded paint work and to create a mix of textures to complete the future-retro design."

Concept Artist Rodney Fuentebella explored ways Star-Lord's helmet would envelop Quill's head. "An earpiece would activate the helmet," he says. "We wanted some effects that would complement the design of the helmet. I thought a light effect would help bridge the transition of the helmet coming from the earpiece."

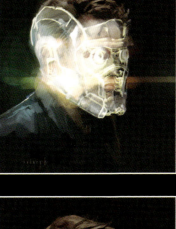

Rodney Fuentebella concept art.

A suggestion from Production Designer Charles Wood helped inspire Concept Artist Chris Rosewarne's designs for Star-Lord's pistols. "He had me call up the *Redbone* song 'Come and Get Your Love,' which is in the scene," Rosewarne says. "Quill is grooving to his cassette player as he moves over the surface of this planet, and he's a bit of a rogue--a bit risky, a bit fun.

"Because it was period music, I thought of 1950s hot rods with exposed engines. So I started doing guns where I pulled some panels off. Quill was a tinkerer who could modify his own equipment."

Chris Rosewarne concept art.

CHAPTER ONE: THE LEGENDARY STAR-LORD

"This is Quill's personal tool kit," Rosewarne says. "An electromagnet, a lock pick and a plasma-glow light ball. The boot-thrusters are an early version, not the one in the film. I had to design something that looked jet-propelled to enable Quill not to fly, but to take bigger jumps or to propel himself a little bit further."

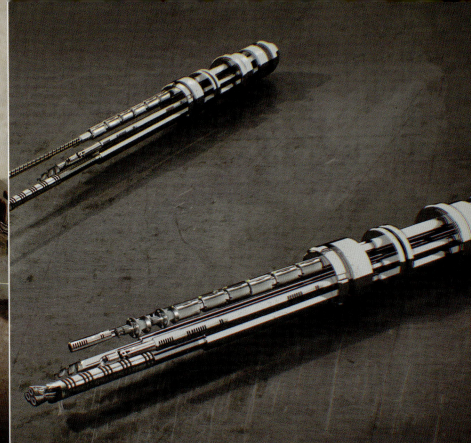

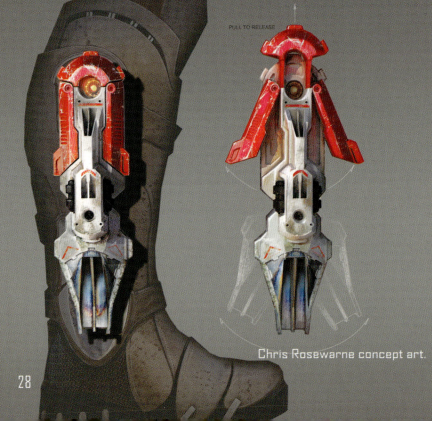

Chris Rosewarne concept art.

Moving Picture Co. concept art.

CHAPTER ONE: THE LEGENDARY STAR-LORD

MORAG
M31V J00443799+4129236

Star-Lord's search for the Orb takes him to an ancient temple on the planet Morag. Charles Wood sent a unit to the White Desert in Egypt to gather visual reference.

"Morag was a dry, blistered, salty, geological world full of crazy rock shapes," Wood says. "The oceans on this planet had receded millennia ago, so it was like a dry seabed type of world, devoid of life."

Visual Effects Supervisor Stephane Ceretti made the long trip south from Cairo to the White Desert. "Its white-stone formations were actually at the bottom of the sea at some point," Ceretti says. "When Charlie built that set in London, we used the stills from Egypt to extend the set."

CHAPTER ONE: THE LEGENDARY STAR-LORD

Kevin Jenkins concept art.

31

"The architecture had been eaten and destroyed, with pools of water like you'd find on a coastline once the tide had gone out." Concept Artist Bob Cheshire says of his take on Morag. "I try to listen to the images, the quiet swish and glugging of the water, possibly through the coral that's grown on some piece of broken architecture… or maybe the coral whistles a bit in the wind? Maybe there's a salty sea smell? It's a useful tool to think more broadly than only the visual because it helps engage your imagination when creating environments."

Justin Sweet keyframe.

CHAPTER ONE: THE LEGENDARY STAR-LORD

Kevin Jenkins concept art (inset).

"Quill uses a device which constructs a moving, 3-D, visual record of Morag before it was destroyed by floods," Cheshire says. "We see how people went about their daily lives before their planet was devastated, covered in meters of silt and debris. The audience and Quill understand that Morag had a sophisticated, evolved culture advanced enough to build dynamic environments—and responsible enough to possess the powerful object Quill seeks."

Bob Cheshire concept art.

Chris Rosewarne concept art.

CHAPTER ONE: THE LEGENDARY STAR-LORD

As the visual language developed, we began to explore a much darker and less expansive space--something more akin to ancient anti-chambers," Cheshire says of the Orb's evolution from warm to colder and broken. "So instantly, with such little light, the space became more claustrophobic; the air a little thicker, less optimistic, more malevolent."

Bob Cheshire concept art with production still (inset).

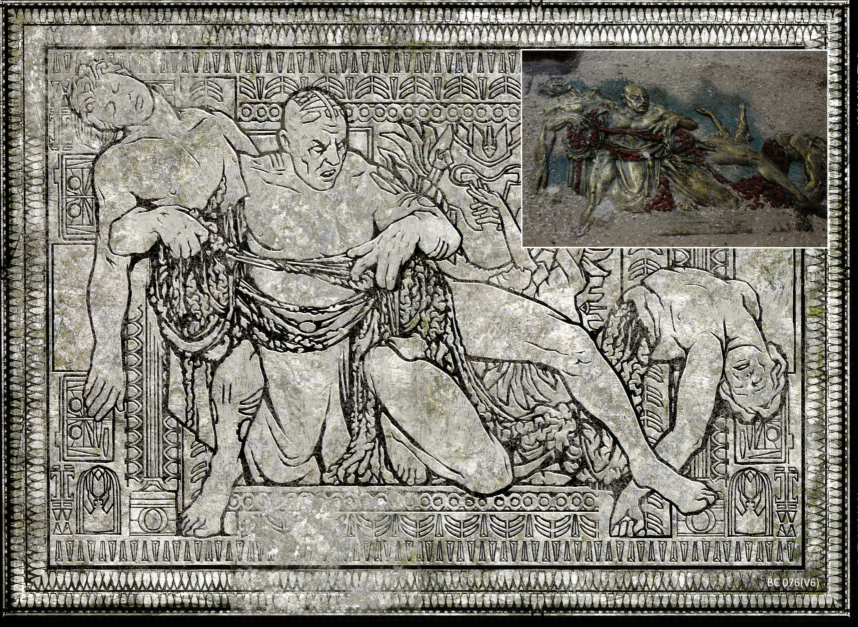

In one of the many intricate carvings covering the Morag temple's walls, the cosmic entities Death, Eternity, Infinity, and Entropy—important supernatural beings in the comic-book Marvel Universe—surround representations of the powerful Infinity Stones.

"We looked at carvings from many cultures," Cheshire says of his design. "But Egyptian hieroglyphics look like Egyptian hieroglyphics, for example, and they are stylistically bound to their culture and to Earth. So while we referenced different cultural designs, we couldn't make it look like any of them. Earlier designs were most alien-like and otherworldly, but too much weirdness stopped the image from being read. It was a question of balance."

Concept art by Bob Cheshire with Oliver Van Der Vijver (inset).

Death embodies decay and can free the soul of a living being. Often taking the form of a woman, Death can manipulate reality, time, and space, and came into existence at the same time as Entropy, Eternity, and Infinity. Immortals are immune to Death's ability. Thanos wanted to rule the universe with Death. To impress her, he killed all life in half the universe with the snap of his fingers.

Entropy came into being at the beginning of time along with his father, Eternity. Entropy's purpose is destruction; this drive pits him in a constant struggle with Eternity, whose goal is creation. Together, they keep the cycles of creation and destruction in balance.

Eternity represents all time in the universe, and has unlimited ability to manipulate time, space, matter energy, or reality. Eternity and Infinity are two of the three essential forces in the universe. They represent necessity, while Death represents vengeance.

Infinity represents all space in the universe. Infinity and Eternity are in constant competition with Death, who attempts to reduce life while Infinity and Eternity expand life. She is the sister of Eternity.

Clockwise from top left: Death, Entropy, Infinity, and Eternity circle the Infinity Stones.

CHAPTER ONE: THE LEGENDARY STAR-LORD

Justin Sweet keyframe.

Concept Artist Justin Sweet illustrated the Orb's legendary power, as wielded by cosmic entity Entropy. "He activates the Orb, and the power crackles forward like flames, destroying everyone nearby," Sweet says. "I liked the contrast of the blue highlights of the black flames against the ash-colored sky."

CHAPTER ONE: THE LEGENDARY STAR-LORD

KORATH

Upon locating the Orb, Star-Lord is confronted by Ronan's enforcer, Korath, and a cadre of Sakaaran soldiers. Costume Illustrator Jack Dudman worked with Alexandra Byrne to create Korath's basic form. Dudman's starting point was Concept Artist Jackson Sze's original designs, which evolved once actor Djimon Hounsou was cast.

"Alex Byrne wanted a really alien-looking surface to the armor," Dudman says. "She found a selection of abstract architecture reference, with forms flowing into each other, and I took my cues from there."

Jack Dudman concept art.

Jackson Sze concept art.

SMUFX test.

CHAPTER ONE: THE LEGENDARY STAR-LORD

Jackson Sze concept art.

Anthony Francisco concept art.

CHAPTER ONE: THE LEGENDARY STAR-LORD

SAKAARAN SOLDIERS

Jerad Marantz concept art.

Concept Artist Jerad Marantz's designs for the Sakaaran soldiers ran the gamut from CG monsters to actor-specific costumes. Once it was determined that the soldiers would be actors, Marantz aimed to create a look that could be mass-produced.

"I decided to do this concept in 3-D," Marantz says. "I find that it helps me resolve the entire design at the same time. You can really explore how these materials fit around the body."

Jerad Marantz concept art.

CHAPTER ONE: THE LEGENDARY STAR-LORD

"Designing a new alien species can be a challenging task without any specifics," Jackson Sze says. Director and Co-Writer James Gunn liked the idea of a skull-like head design reminiscent of World War II German headgear. "The emotional response one gets from skulls and Nazi helmets can be strong," Sze continues. "Our task is to make something that feels alien and unique but with human connections."

Jackson Sze concept art.

Anthony Francisco concept art.

Jackson Sze concept art.

CHAPTER ONE: THE LEGENDARY STAR-LORD

"The Sakaaran soldiers were quite complicated," Alexandra Byrne says. "Their armor is related to their spaceships, their warcraft. And the armor is made from material that they grow on their planet, so it's a mixture of organic matter and clothing."

Justin Sweet concept art.

"With this version of the Sakaaran, I was trying make them feel like an undead army," Concept Artist Anthony Francisco says. "I wanted the armor to seem alive though weathered through years of battles. Thanos is all about death and destruction, and that needed to come across."

Anthony Francisco concept art.

CHAPTER ONE: THE LEGENDARY STAR-LORD

"Each alien character had to look and feel totally believable—as if they could inhabit their world, their environment, without question," says Special Makeup Effects Designer David White, who oversaw a team of more than 100 technical artists in the workshop and about 60 on set designing and creating practical prosthetics for dozens of alien species.

"The Sakaaran soldiers were only seen with prosthetics for closeup, select shots," White says. "We sculpted up a full-head prosthetic mask, which had many different material textures and colors. We also created prosthetic gloves for their hands."

Charlie Wen concept art.

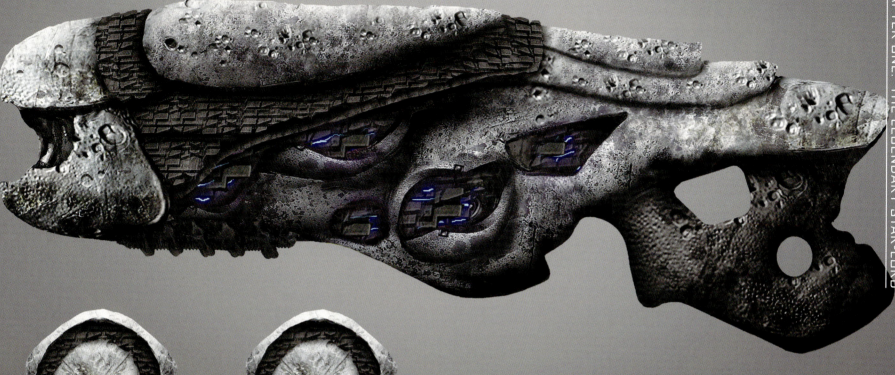

NECRO RIFLE

Christopher Caldow concept art.

THE MILANO

"For me, the Milano is another character in the film," Concept Artist Roberto Fernández Castro says. "I tried to think about its personality and how the design could help to tell the story. Here, the Milano is in action showing all its power. The vessel was bird-shaped, agile, but heavy and tough at the same time. This image is the final piece that concludes hours and hours of hard work. The model that 3-D Set Designer Gregory Fangeaux made was a perfect starting point for this image."

Roberto Fernández Castro concept art.

CHAPTER ONE: THE LEGENDARY STAR-LORD

55

Star-Lord's ship was one of the bigger builds on set—"a super-cool spaceship right out of Charlie Wood's brain," as Jonathan Schwartz says.

Wood's design process is very art-intensive, according to Jeremy Latcham. "He's incredibly prolific," Latcham explains. "The way he works is he iterates and iterates and iterates and gives you a huge swath of material to choose from right up front—giving you every idea you might want to explore, and then we start narrowing."

Wood wanted the Milano to echo Quill's character. "James wanted a set you would walk into and grin, in a boyish sort of way," Wood says.

CHAPTER ONE: THE LEGENDARY STAR-LORD

Roberto Fernández Castro concept art.

"The Milano is part of the Ravager culture," James Gunn says. "Normally, we see technology and progress in science-fiction movies, but the Ravagers are guys who love muscle cars. The sensation of touch is important to them. So even though there are ways to make a spaceship that doesn't tremble, they want to feel the trembling. They want the tactile sensation of feeling their hands on the buttons, to feel everything they're interacting with."

Roberto Fernández Castro concept art.

Roberto Fernández Castro concept art.

Paul Catling concept art.

CHAPTER ONE: THE LEGENDARY STAR-LORD

"Concept Artist Roberto Fernández Castro's architectural background was a perfect fit for designing the Milano spacecraft in enough detail to be built as full-scale sets," says Atomhawk Design's Director Ron Ashtiani. "Castro worked with Atomhawk until the last two months of production, when he finished up as a freelancer."

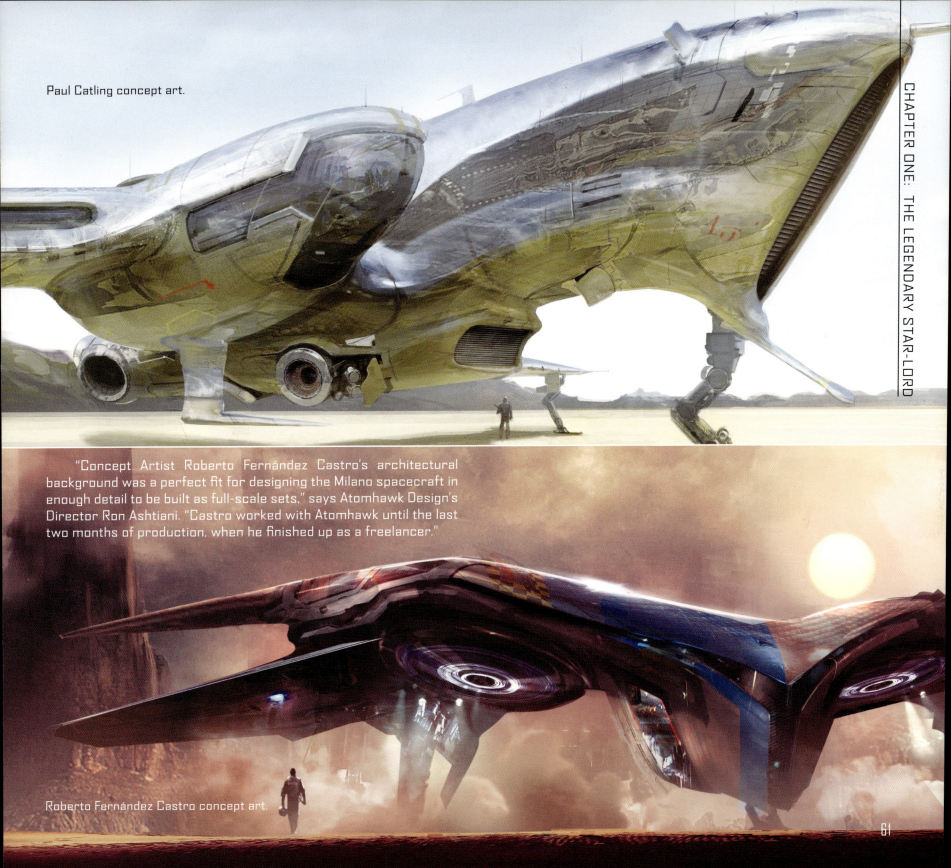

Roberto Fernández Castro concept art.

"I think that the underside of the Milano is as beautiful as the top," Castro says. "Four huge disc-shaped engines give a strong personality to the spaceship."

Roberto Fernández Castro concept art.

Dan Walker concept art.

Roberto Fernández Castro concept art.

CHAPTER ONE: THE LEGENDARY STAR-LORD

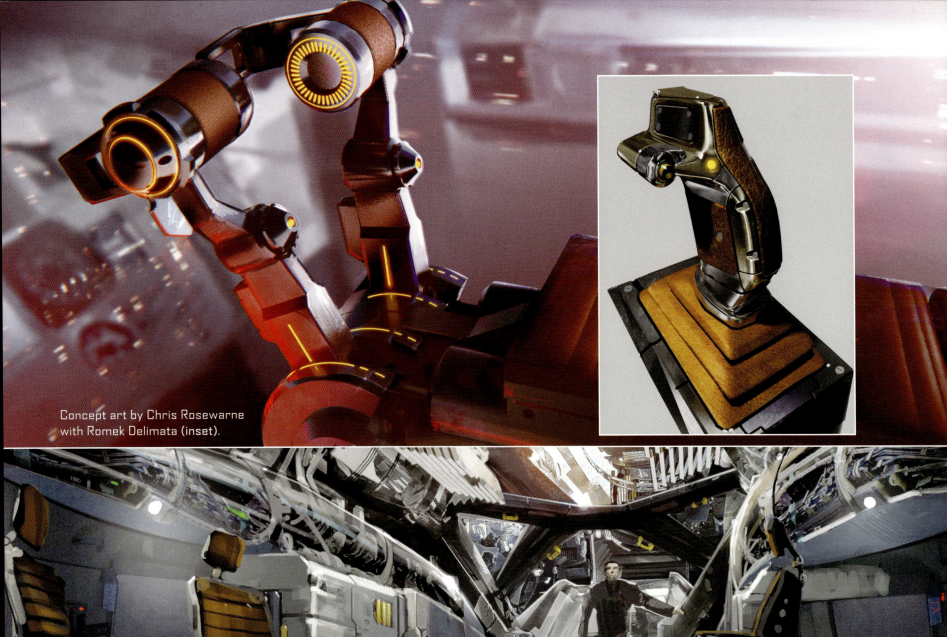

Concept art by Chris Rosewarne with Romek Delimata (inset).

"The Milano's controls had to make you want to run your hands over them," Chris Rosewarne says. "Concept Artist Romek Delimata's design for the joystick looked and felt like a 1970s metal lighter, something polished just through being handled a lot. The spaceship was comfortable yet cool, with a slight retro feel. It mirrored Quill's personality."

Romek Delimata concept art.

Delimata, a pilot who previously owned a flight-simulator business, brought a level of plausibility to the Milano. "I spent a lot of time down in the prop room, sourcing bits and pieces of aircraft junk I thought would be usable for set dressing and design."

Rosewarne was also inspired by trips to the prop workshop. "It was like getting in touch with your inner kid," he says. "You'd hold stuff in your hand and think it could be a thruster or a raygun. You could get your hands on stuff that looked real or felt real."

Romek Delimata concept art.

Delimata was leaning toward shag-pile carpets, but Wood's input changed his approach. "The thinking we came up with was that maybe the Milano was some kind of military vehicle that Quill had gotten hold of," Delimata says. "He'd made it his own so it has a rawness to the interior, as well as bits that make it more comfortable for him."

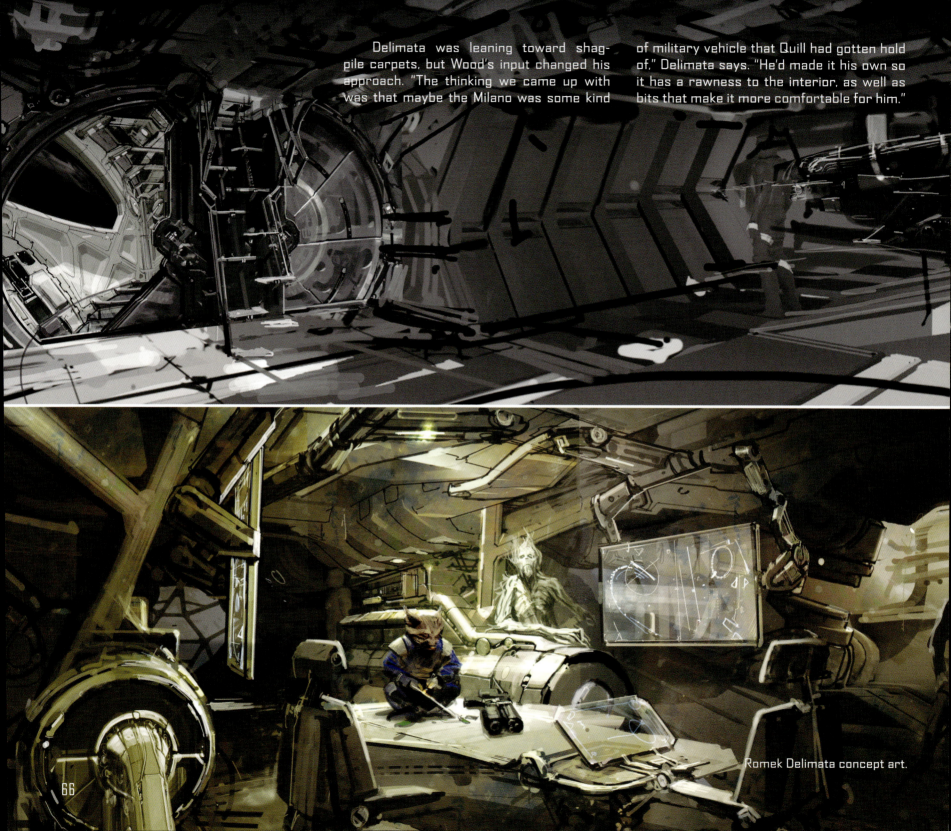

Romek Delimata concept art.

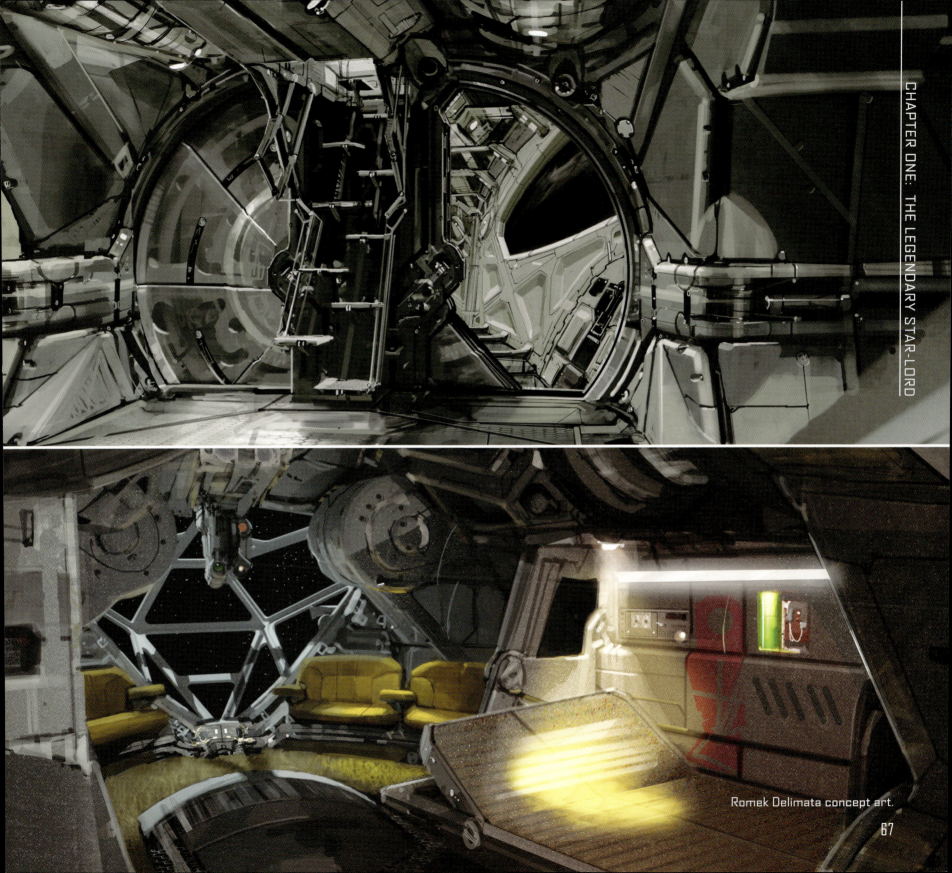

CHAPTER ONE: THE LEGENDARY STAR-LORD

Romek Delimata concept art.

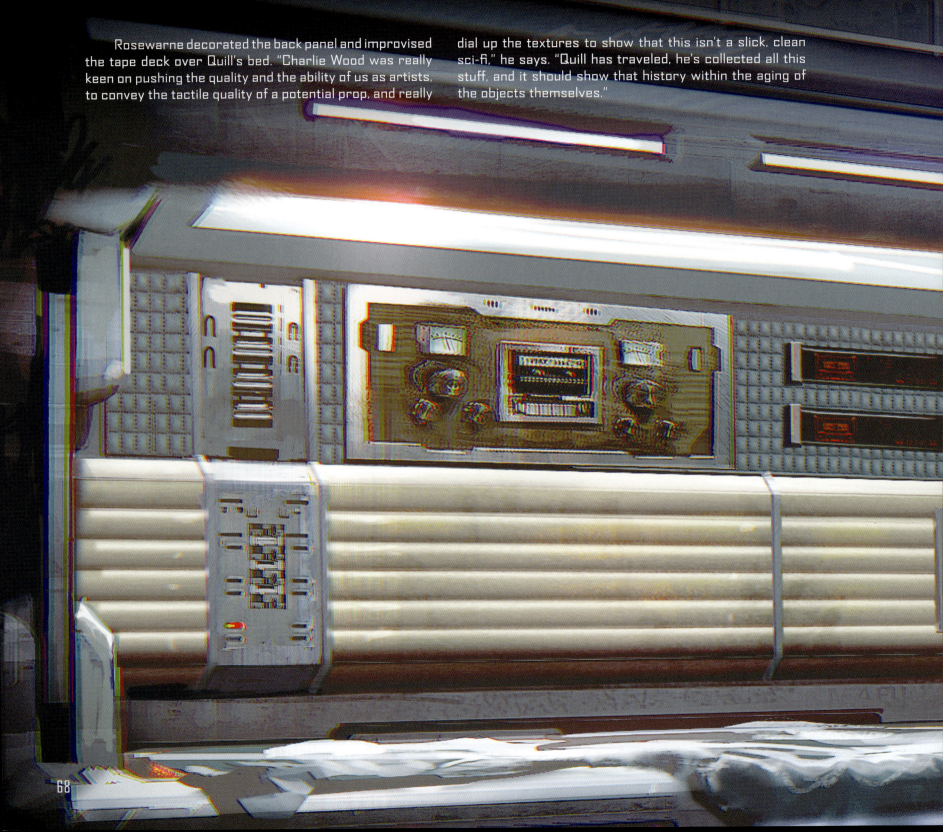

Rosewarne decorated the back panel and improvised the tape deck over Quill's bed. "Charlie Wood was really keen on pushing the quality and the ability of us as artists, to convey the tactile quality of a potential prop, and really dial up the textures to show that this isn't a slick, clean sci-fi," he says. "Quill has traveled, he's collected all this stuff, and it should show that history within the aging of the objects themselves."

Chris Rosewarne concept art.

CHAPTER TWO
DARK ALLIANCES

Paul Catling concept art.

The swashbuckling, colorful world of Star-Lord and the Milano takes a dark and heavy turn with the appearance of Ronan and his imposing Dark Aster.

"Drawing concepts with few parameters is scary at the best of times, but being tasked to make something truly original can be terrifying," Concept Artist Paul Catling says of the menacing spacecraft. "Charlie Wood put together reference he liked—images of rusting, greasy submarines; aircraft carriers; and cathedral-like, abstract renderings of hell."

Ronan's ship proved more difficult to realize than Quill's, according to Production Designer Charles Wood.

"In a sense, the Milano was the safer world for us because it was a rocket ship, something we're familiar with," Wood says. "The Dark Aster was a much darker world—it was based on coal dust. It was so abstract."

Though seen on screen in eight different configurations, only a portion of the Dark Aster was built on set.

"That was a big production challenge in terms of how to retrofit the one stage so that it didn't look like the same space over and over again, and so that it actually played as every different part of this giant ship," Co-Producer Jonathan Schwartz says.

The monolithic, lumbering craft moves slowly through space, laboring under its own weight and pumping soot into the galaxy.

"The bad guys have a polluting exhaust when they put the thrusters on," Visual Effects Supervisor Stephane Ceretti says. "Dark, black smoke comes out of their thrusters. They're not very responsible. Those are the kind of little things we think about just to add character."

DARK ASTER

Catling remembers being disappointed in his first designs. "Then, Charlie said it should be made from concrete, which conjured up notions of the impenetrable, but the problem now was to make it seem like a spaceship and not a floating building," Catling says.

He experimented with twisting and scaling concrete slab shapes in 3-D. "The idea that it was totally un-aerodynamic and brutish made sense somehow. We took a break from the exterior for a few months to work on the interior, and later refined the shape of the wings and how they morphed into the main body to make the ship more elegant and unified."

Paul Catling concept art.

CHAPTER TWO: DARK ALLIANCES

"We had a fantastic team of four artists with strong sci-fi backgrounds working on the movie for around eight months," Atomhawk Design's Director Ron Ashtiani says. "In addition to Roberto Fernández Castro, we had Tim Hill, who is a speed painter and quickly developed ideas. He has a great eye for mood and lighting. Pete Thompson is superb at capturing action and focused on key story images. Stuart Ellis was working on weapons/prop design."

Tim Hill concept art.

CHAPTER TWO: DARK ALLIANCES

Tim Hill concept art.

75

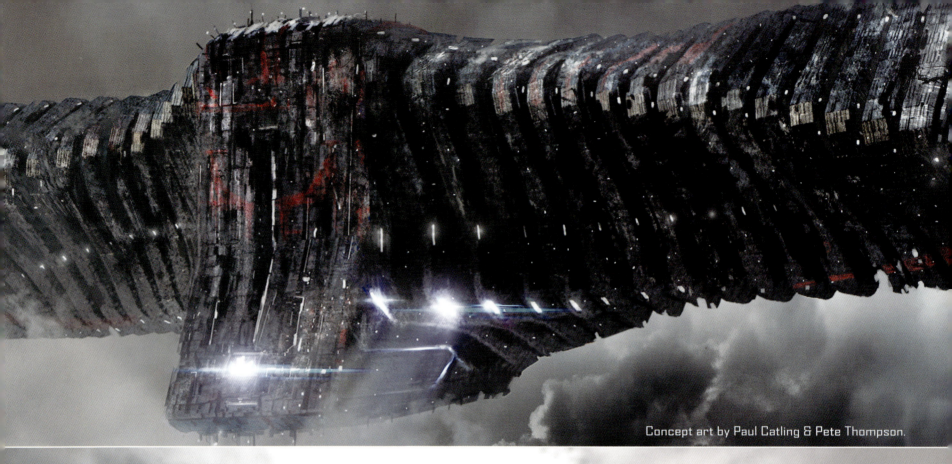

Concept art by Paul Catling & Pete Thompson.

The team brought the 3-D ship models together, at which point they realized the Dark Aster was 1.5 miles across. "This seemed ludicrous, and we looked at bringing it down to a more manageable size," Catling says. "But when I started working on a rough animation of the Milano flying through the interior of the Dark Aster wings, its journey was over in seconds, so the ship had to be scaled back up to its original 1.5 miles."

Paul Catling concept art.

CHAPTER TWO: DARK ALLIANCES

"This design combined a bone-like structure with insectoid-like armoring to give a highly organic look to the ship." Concept Artist Tim Hill says.

Tim Hill concept art.

DARK ASTER FLIGHT DECK

As impressive as it was, even the set for the Dark Aster's flight deck at Shepperton Studios had its limits. "It couldn't include everything," Concept Artist Bob Cheshire says. "So a group of concepts were created that explored beyond the boundaries of the set—including what the outward view along the length of the flight deck to space beyond looked like, or taking in the enormous height of the ceiling. This visual looks back at the throne and the Sakaaran pilots."

Bob Cheshire concept art.

Anthony Francisco concept art.

CHAPTER TWO: DARK ALLIANCES

Bob Cheshire concept art.

CHAPTER TWO: DARK ALLIANCES

NECROCRAFT

"It had to be alien but also recognizable as a three-man cockpit," Paul Catling says of the Necrocraft interior, which had to match Tim Hill's exterior. "The problem was it couldn't have the dials, buttons, and consoles that normally inform an audience that this is a cockpit. But without them, it becomes just a flying room.

"I tried putting a cockpit within a cockpit by referencing 1950s Formula 1 cars and surrounded these pods with a very un-ergonomic, 'ankle-snapping' space—layers of sharp, laser-cut steel plate that perhaps acts as a circuit board channeling power to the pods. The voids in the floor and walls were an attempt to regain the visual complexity lost by omitting the dials and buttons."

CHAPTER TWO: DARK ALLIANCES

"The process of rapidly producing a wide range of design explorations and purging any preconceptions you might have is very important," Tim Hill says.

Tim Hill concept art.

83

Tim Hill concept art.

CHAPTER TWO: DARK ALLIANCES

Stephane Ceretti sought to give a unique feel to the Necrocraft's movements. "Our main reference was a slow-motion document about how flies move, how they fly, and how they change direction. It was interesting to see. We wanted to make them a bit more insect-like, so they could spin and have very sharp turns that you wouldn't get on a fighter plane."

RONAN'S CHAMBERS

The set for Ronan's chambers already had been designed when Concept Artist Chris Rosewarne illustrated the director's idea of Ronan emerging from a pool of black liquid that drains away from him. "He leaves all these umbilical-style cords basically stuck into his body, so that he looks like a porcupine with tubes coming out of him," Rosewarne says.

Chris Rosewarne concept art.

CHAPTER TWO: DARK ALLIANCES

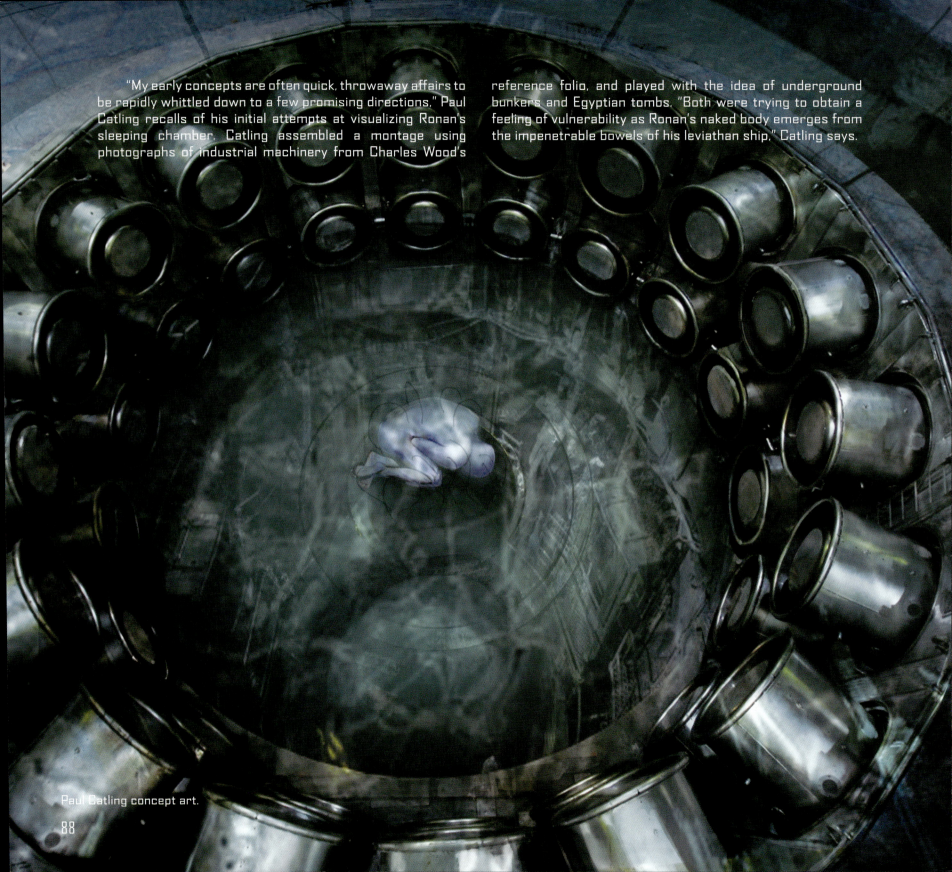

"My early concepts are often quick, throwaway affairs to be rapidly whittled down to a few promising directions," Paul Catling recalls of his initial attempts at visualizing Ronan's sleeping chamber. Catling assembled a montage using photographs of industrial machinery from Charles Wood's reference folio, and played with the idea of underground bunkers and Egyptian tombs. "Both were trying to obtain a feeling of vulnerability as Ronan's naked body emerges from the impenetrable bowels of his leviathan ship," Catling says.

Paul Catling concept art.

Paul Catling concept art.

Jack Dudman concept art.

Special Make-Up Effects Designer David White's team created multiple prosthetic makeups for the Exolon Monks, including contact lenses with spiral pupils. "They are serene and spiritual—with pale, waxen-like alien skin," he says.

Prosthetic Make-up by Special Make-Up Effects.

CHAPTER TWO: DARK ALLIANCES

89

RONAN

Ronan is a powerful extremist who has broken from his Kree race. "He really doesn't like weakness," Executive Producer Jeremy Latcham says. "He wants a world where the weakest have been pushed aside and only the strongest survive, and that'll be the best society."

Charlie Wen concept art.

"James had specified that he wanted to make Ronan feel like he was a corrupt, religious extremist," Marvel Studios Head of Visual Development Charlie Wen says. "Taking those words, I began drawing influences from Egyptian pharaohs, with draping headpieces, which felt equally ceremonial and warrior-like."

Charlie Wen concept art.

Andy Park concept art.

CHAPTER TWO: DARK ALLIANCES

91

"Utilizing face paint, I gave him markings that felt more ominous than holy and textures that felt dark, much like the world he is coming from," Wen says.

Charlie Wen concept art.

"Ronan's Cosmi-rod is originally from the comics, and had to show strength and the ability to cast a charge of energy out to crush his enemies," Property Master Barry Gibbs says. "We tried many different designs to produce something that was quite elegant and beautiful although powerful, and we put in a lot of effort to stop it from looking like Thor's Mjolnir. We were also given the task of showing that it had an internal strength. We were able to place a light source to create a sense of this power, but ultimately this had to become a visual-effects element."

Dan Walker concept art.

Justin Sweet concept art.

CHAPTER TWO: DARK ALLIANCES

In his quest to cull the unfit, Ronan strikes a deal with Thanos. The mighty warlord agrees to destroy the Nova Corps—protectors of the weak—in exchange for the Orb.

"What is revealed later in the course of the film is the Orb contains a powerful Infinity Stone," Executive Producer and Marvel Studios Co-President Louis D'Esposito says. "Ronan defies Thanos once he becomes influenced by its power."

Justin Sweet concept art.

CHAPTER TWO: DARK ALLIANCES

SANCTUARY
N5X2 106311411+2123518

Loïc e338 Zimmermann concept art.

"Ronan is summoned to Thanos to report his progress, but he gets caught up in a violent argument" Concept Artist Loic e338 Zimmermann says. "The central idea was that Thanos is living among the remains of a destroyed planet that he conquered. He stands high above everyone else in the image, gazing at a distant galaxy. Most of the elements in the composition are leaning or pointing in his direction to establish him as the absolute force ruling over this world. To depict Thanos in all his glory, I gathered reference of various ruins, along with the concepts from Charlie Wen."

CHAPTER TWO: DARK ALLIANCES

THANOS

"After being teased in *Marvel's The Avengers* as that purple-chinned profile that turned to the camera and smiled in mid-credits, Thanos' role is becoming a little more clear," Louis D'Esposito says.

Comic-book writer and artist Jim Starlin created Thanos in the pages of *Iron Man* in 1973, before the Marvel Cinematic Universe's Peter Quill was even born. "Thanos started off as just another villain," Starlin says. "Then I realized I could channel all the vile and evil things that lurk within me through him and onto the printed page. Made life easier for my cats."

Charlie Wen was determined to maintain the epic proportions of the comic-book Thanos. "He is a Titan," Wen says. "He needs to feel threatening and imposing while also maintaining a regal persona."

Thanos is often defined by his obsession with both the female embodiment of the entity Death and the omnipotent Infinity Stones.

Thanos is not always ruthless, and his motives can be difficult for humans to understand. In the Cinematic Universe, he adopted and raised both Nebula and Gamora.

"Much the same way the Guardians all become family, here's a guy on the other side of the universe who's attracting all these other people," Jeremy Latcham says. "Except instead of bringing out the best in each other, they're bringing out the worst. And so he's raising this group of people with Ronan, Korath, Gamora, and Nebula. Kind of like the evil Manson Family version of the Guardians."

Charlie Wen concept art.

Charlie Wen concept art.

CHAPTER TWO: DARK ALLIANCES

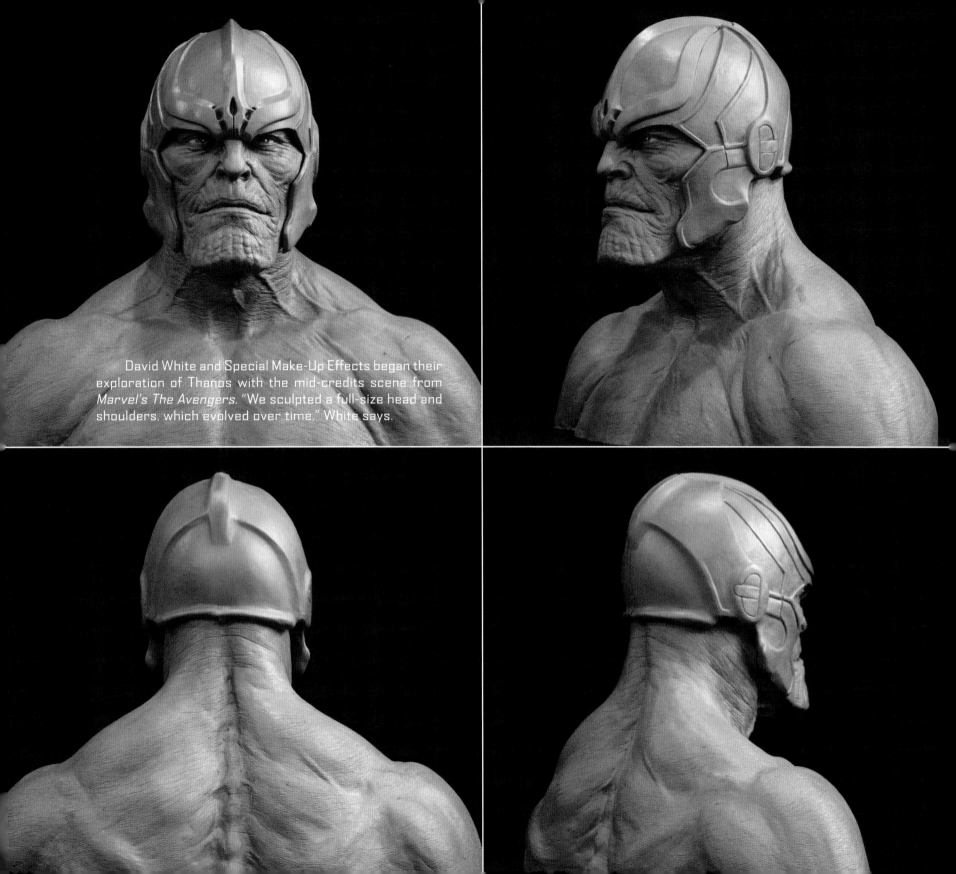

David White and Special Make-Up Effects began their exploration of Thanos with the mid-credits scene from *Marvel's The Avengers*. "We sculpted a full-size head and shoulders, which evolved over time," White says.

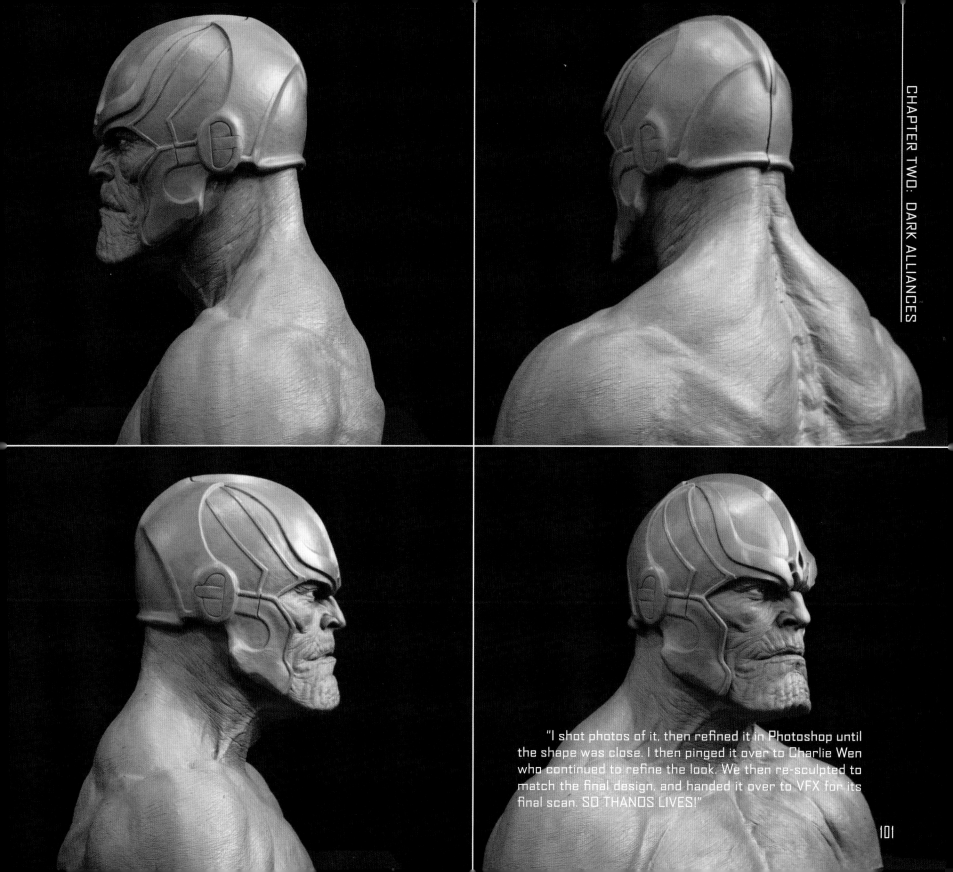

"I shot photos of it, then refined it in Photoshop until the shape was close. I then pinged it over to Charlie Wen who continued to refine the look. We then re-sculpted to match the final design, and handed it over to VFX for its final scan. SO THANOS LIVES!"

"This was a keyframe that I actually did for *Marvel's The Avengers*," Concept Artist Andy Park says. "It's the reveal moment where the fans go, 'OMG! It's Thanos!' And the non-fans go, 'Who's that purple guy?' I'm a self-proclaimed Marvel fan, and I couldn't believe I was painting this character even as I was painting it."

Andy Park keyframe.

CHAPTER TWO: DARK ALLIANCES

NEBULA

From his experience with Red Skull on Marvel's *Captain America: The First Avenger*, David White knew he and SMUFX would have to shave actress Karen Gillan's head for her role as Nebula.

"That may seem a little radical, but it had to be done to get the skull to look slick and in proportion to the rest of her body," White says. "Shaving the head also means a reduced time in the makeup chair, plus less touchup time on set."

Andy Park concept art.

CHAPTER TWO: DARK ALLIANCES

Because he always strives to retain the actor's features, White found Nebula's biomechanical look difficult to execute.

"Her real skin is only visible under the chin, neck, top lip, and ears," he says. "There is a layer of biomechanical stencils and a bold color palette that bridges the gap between the two. We used a different material for the tech on her head and mechanical arm. It's a dense foam that restricts movement, making it more believable as a hard casing. Only areas around the eye and joints in the arm are more flexible, for safety and practicality.

"Nebula was a hundred percent SMUFX, a real challenge."

Andy Park concept art.

Justin Sweet concept art.

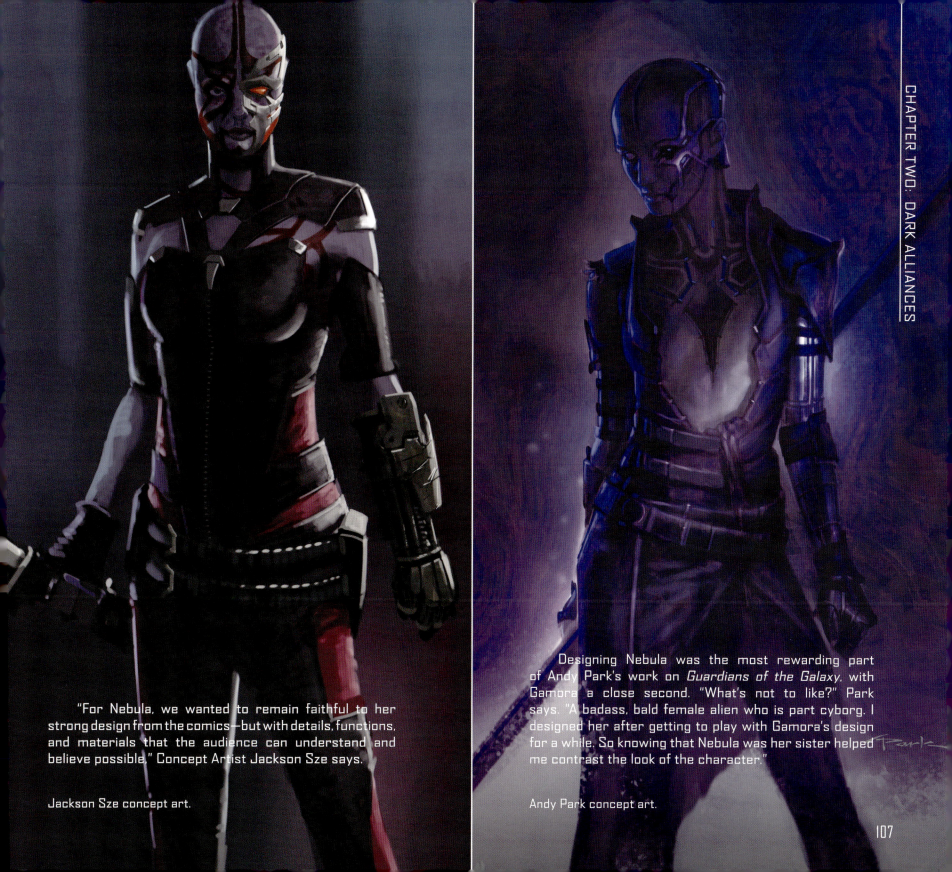

CHAPTER TWO: DARK ALLIANCES

"For Nebula, we wanted to remain faithful to her strong design from the comics—but with details, functions, and materials that the audience can understand and believe possible," Concept Artist Jackson Sze says.

Jackson Sze concept art.

Designing Nebula was the most rewarding part of Andy Park's work on *Guardians of the Galaxy*, with Gamora a close second. "What's not to like?" Park says. "A badass, bald female alien who is part cyborg. I designed her after getting to play with Gamora's design for a while. So knowing that Nebula was her sister helped me contrast the look of the character."

Andy Park concept art.

107

CHAPTER THREE

GALAXY'S MOST WANTED

Once Star-Lord acquires the Orb and escapes from Korath, he flies the Milano from Morag to Xandar, where he plans to sell the Orb to a broker of antiques and artifacts.

The environments of Xandar and Morag are completely different from one another, and from planets still to come; each had to be imagined, designed, and executed before sooting could begin. But the view from space was only the first step.

"The geographical concepts are big worlds you see from eight... ten...20,000 feet up in the air looking down onto them. Then you have to get down on to the ground and walk through them, and then you have to go within them," Production Designer Charles Wood says.

Costume Designer Alexandra Byrne's team developed detailed notes for each planet. "Once you get into production, everybody's so busy that things can get messy unless you have a framework," Byrne says. "We note what species live there, what kind of society it is, how that society works, what the climate is like, what kind of citizens there are, is it friendly, is it a toxic atmosphere, what's the role of men and women, what's the family unit, how many generations live together, what's the lifespan, is there obesity? Are people perfected? Do they have shortsighted people? Everything you put on screen should go toward helping to tell that story."

XANDAR
M31V J00442326+412708

Artists illustrated slice-of-life looks at the city streets of the film's planets, demonstrating the diversity of the alien societies the Art Department had created. Concept Artist Andy Park painted human-looking aliens alongside other types of beings on the Xandar Mall. "This was another moment where I was amazed that Marvel was doing a movie like this," Park says. "Much respect!"

CHAPTER THREE: GALAXY'S MOST WANTED

Andy Park keyframe.

Concept art by Nigel Booth, Colin Shulver & David White/SMUFX.

Luke Fisher/SMUFX concept art.

Concept art by Howard Swindell & David White/SMUFX.

Paul Catling concept art.

Jack Dudman concept art.

CHAPTER THREE: GALAXY'S MOST WANTED

Jackson Sze keyframe.

Warren Holder concept art.

TI'ASHA

Costume Illustrator Jack Dudman adapted and colored Costume Illustrator Darrell Warner's ideas for Ti'Asha and Bereet, based on input from Alexandra Byrne.

Jack Dudman concept art.

BEREET

ALIEN BROKER

"Being a high-end art dealer requires a business suit audiences can relate to, but alien enough in its cuts to be a little surprising," Jackson Sze says.

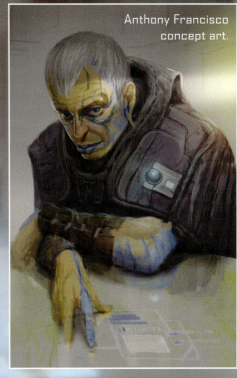

Anthony Francisco concept art.

Anthony Francisco concept art.

Jackson Sze concept art.

CHAPTER THREE: GALAXY'S MOST WANTED

ROCKET

Two-and-a-half-foot tall Rocket, a biogenetically engineered raccoon, was computer-generated—as was his best friend, Groot.

"In the beginning, we had two vendors: Framestore doing Rocket, and MPC doing Groot," Executive Producer and EVP of VFX and Post-Production Victoria Alonso says. "But then we realized that was going to be a nightmare, and they both started doing everything together."

Charlie Wen concept art.

CHAPTER THREE: GALAXY'S MOST WANTED

How do you bring a gun-toting, talking raccoonoid to life? Not easily, according to Visual Effects Supervisor Stephane Ceretti. "Rocket needs to talk, but he's a raccoon, so you have to make that feel real, and he's got a huge breadth of expression," Ceretti says. "So that's the challenge for Rocket—the overall acting. And the fur."

Charlie Wen concept art.

Ryan Meinerding concept art.

"Director and Co-Writer James Gunn was keen on wanting Rocket to emote, while simultaneously retaining his distinct characteristics and not turning into a caricature," Marvel Studios Head of Visual Development Charlie Wen says. "We needed to find a blend of anthropomorphic characteristics as well as typical raccoon quirks to bring Rocket to life and give him his due."

Charlie Wen concept art.

"James Gunn was kind enough to bring in a live raccoon for us to study," says Concept Artist Iain McCaig, who also studied video reference. "I was fascinated by how much they rely on their hands, so I tried to let Rocket's hands lead the way."

"The pencil sketches were my early attempts to feel what it was like to be Rocket, to put him on and dance around in his shoes—or paws," McCaig says.

Iain McCaig concept art.

CHAPTER THREE: GALAXY'S MOST WANTED

"Visual Development would send illustrations over, then the prop guys would start designing guns, illustrating them into his hands," Executive Producer Jeremy Latcham says. "The images went back and forth, making sure the gun they put in his hands didn't undermine his proportions. It had to be big enough to be funny, but not too big to make him feel small."

Moving Picture Co. concept art.

CHAPTER THREE: GALAXY'S MOST WANTED

"Rocket has a signature rifle," Property Master Barry Gibbs says. "Initially, it was purely a visual effect, and so was not going to be necessary to actually make. But as the film progressed, we realized that we required an in-camera prop which could be used for visual-effects lighting reference and for a set-decoration requirement. The initial design was created by MPC, which we then translated into a functional 3-D model. This was then 3-D printed, plated, and hand-finished in-house to give it durability for set use."

Moving Picture Co. design with Props Department model.

"The challenge was the more expressive Rocket became, the cartoonier it seemed to make him," Wen says. "Ultimately, the elements that made him look genuinely tough and serious were born from performance—his gestures, the way he carried himself, his voice and stance, and the ease with which he used a gun twice the size of himself."

Charlie Wen concept art.

CHAPTER THREE: GALAXY'S MOST WANTED

Justin Sweet concept art.

Jackson Sze concept art.

Special Make-Up Effects Designer David White's team built a stuffed Rocket, then Alex Byrne and her Costume Design department created its clothing.

"It was incredible watching it all come together as the different departments collaborated," Latcham says. "And then at the same time, visual-effects vendors started building a model and putting it through a walk cycle. Meanwhile, James gave incredibly detailed notes about how he wanted Rocket to move. And we did a ton of research looking at different snouts, different ears, different fur. It took months and months and months to land on the guy that is our Rocket."

Moving Picture Co. concept art.

GROOT

"Concept Artist Josh Herman cracked Groot, early on," Jeremy Latcham says. "He immediately got in the ballpark after a couple of weeks of meetings. Josh works in 3-D, so there was quickly a model that could be moved around and posed."

Josh Herman concept art.

Groot had to appear capable of fluid movement. "He couldn't have one limb be a whole branch, because it would be cracking and breaking, so we started looking at twisted trees and trees with a lot of vines and roots," Herman says.

"The model was passed on to David White's team, and they built a maquette," Latcham says. "They captured the essence of Groot, the eyes and emotion Josh and Charlie had designed in Groot's face, and that then became the on-set representation of Groot. We photographed it in the lighting for the animators and visual-effects companies, and then that got passed on to Visual Effects."

CHAPTER THREE: GALAXY'S MOST WANTED

Herman studied carved wooden masks to craft Groot's face. "I started out sculpting something in ZBrush with those ideas in mind, and came up with vines and roots acting like musculature," he says. "But Groot still had some harder wooden plates that make up most of his body. In the comics, he had long branches sticking out of his head, so I tried something like that—but tying them into his head, as well."

Josh Herman concept art.

"A gentle giant, a fierce warrior, an inquisitive child," Jackson Sze says of the different approaches he tried for Groot. "The most interesting ones were *not* about him being a warrior. A sensitive soul who is capable of immense destruction seems the most interesting. I can imagine him plucking flowers out of his own body to admire, shortly before Rocket orders him to attack. Playing with eye placements, pupil designs, and mouth shapes significantly altered the attitude of Groot each time."

"I once had the idea of Groot being allergic to the flowers growing all over his body, and he had to constantly preen himself lest he sneezes uncontrollably. Alas the idea did not take...root," Sze says.

Jackson Sze concept art.

"We wanted Groot to feel young as a character, to convey an endearing sense of naiveté and wide-eyed awe of the world," Charlie Wen says.

Charlie Wen concept art.

CHAPTER THREE: GALAXY'S MOST WANTED

Visual Development artists experimented with different proportions, head shapes, and "haircuts." "We found some new things we liked, such as a head done by Jackson, and we incorporated those things back into mine for the final design," Herman says.

Anthony Francisco concept art.

131

"Groot is about seven feet tall," Victoria Alonso says. "On set, we had a mask on a stick with a seven-feet marker."

Jackson Sze concept art.

A mime also was used on set. "He wore a big Groot helmet so he could be the proper height," Co-Producer Jonathan Schwartz says. "And James' brother Sean stood in for Rocket. We'd run through scenes a couple of times with these stand-ins."

Andy Park concept art.

"When working with Josh Herman, we were continually trying to find a balance between being tree-like and being creature-like," Wen says. "There is a fine line when blending anatomical pieces—like that of a human—with sloping shapes and unique form lines that don't feel human at all. There is where we found our Groot."

Charlie Wen concept art.

CHAPTER THREE: GALAXY'S MOST WANTED

GAMORA

Jack Dudman worked up his Gamora designs with Alex Byrne, adapting lines by Darrell Warner. "We were trying to lock down her makeup," Dudman says. "So with help from the Hair and Makeup department, and looking back at the designs Charlie's team had done, we got a more finalized version with the pink hair and her face markings. This helped sell her punky attitude. Gamora needed to be able to walk down the street and people give her a wide berth."

Jack Dudman concept art.

CHAPTER THREE: GALAXY'S MOST WANTED

Andy Park concept art.

"I wanted to create a look that was both 'out there' and yet still beautiful," Andy Park says. "I played with everything from her skin color to skin texture, hair designs to various tattoos and markings. She is one of the deadliest assassin warriors in the galaxy, so she needed to look formidable and not too delicate. But her vulnerability was necessary to her look, as well. I was very happy when I found out that Zoe Saldana was cast. She perfectly achieves both these qualities."

Andy Park concept art.

Jackson Sze concept art.

Charlie Wen concept art.

Andy Park concept art.

Andy Park concept art.

CHAPTER THREE: GALAXY'S MOST WANTED

"The goal was to find a way to blend technology with flesh in an elegant way—that also didn't feel like it was competing with Nebula," Charlie Wen says of his initial biomechanical approach. "This turned out to be extremely hard to achieve from a practical standpoint, so we turned our attention to a more primal look."

Charlie Wen concept art.

CHAPTER THREE: GALAXY'S MOST WANTED

"Swords are always a problem," Byrne says. "The scale of Gamora's sword would really affect how she moved, so it was decided to have her blade able to enlarge. Zoe is not a big woman, so where do you set the weapon? How does she carry her weapon? It's a big part of working out her look."

Charlie Wen concept art.

Charlie Wen concept art.

CHAPTER THREE: GALAXY'S MOST WANTED

143

"I did these paintovers on a prosthetic sculpt by David White to test the Gamora makeup and look," Park says. White frequently uses early prosthetic photos as base plates for exploring makeup. "This is a stand-in actress," Park continues. "I did a lot more exploration than is shown here on what Zoe Saldana might look like as Gamora. Ultimately, we decided to go with a more minimal approach to her makeup and prosthetics."

Andy Park paintovers.

"James Gunn had a pretty clear idea of what he wanted with this scene," Jackson Sze says. "It is a very specific story moment, so the poses and placements were pretty much set from the get-go. The main gag here is that Groot's arms were chopped off."

Jackson Sze keyframe.

CHAPTER FOUR
CORPS VALUES

Olivier Pron concept art.

Home to the intergalactic peacekeeping force known as the Nova Corps, Xandar was one of only a few environments in the film referenced from physical sources.

"We looked at atoll islands—the Great Barrier Reef, for instance—and a lot of the islands off the Australian coast and the Bahamas from the air," Production Designer Charles Wood says. "That gave us a particular look and feel for the oceans of this watery world with its great big sand dunes and atolls. And that was the basis for the look of the colors and the light of the place. We built an architectural world into that.

"We looked at a lot of satellite imagery for algae blooms and things growing within water—it gives a strange kind of iridescent look to it. We wanted beauty within the film—we were trying to put so many things into an hour and a half of filmmaking. There was never a moment where it was hard to find new material."

Concept Artist Olivier Pron designed a city in the shape of the Nova Corps logo. "Once we narrowed the city outline down to a couple of versions, we started the process of bringing this environment dominated by water to life," Pron says.

"We focused on building areas that would predominately be seen in the film," Pron says. "The mall would be where the main characters would meet for the first time, and the Nova Corps memorial where the final battle is fought would not be too far away. Charles Wood wanted to mix large public spaces and sprawling, manicured gardens with more industrial structures, such as shipyards and dockyards. The idea was that inhabitants could be in or very close to heavy industrial structures while still being surrounded by lush, exotic gardens."

Olivier Pron concept art.

CHAPTER FOUR: CORPS VALUES

Olivier Pron concept art.

CHAPTER FOUR: CORPS VALUES

Pron considered how Xandar's inhabitants would live and feed themselves, as well as their means of transportation and methods of energy production.

"During the process of answering those questions, the setting evolved into a low-rise city filled with gardens," he says. "We avoided the typical 'sci-fi-skyscraper' look. For the energy, we came up with huge maelstroms that the inhabitants tap for their energy needs, adding a spectacular element when seen from above. Xandar being a water world, the obvious choice for food production was algae farms, allowing us to create large colorful algae around Xandar. To add drama to the city skyline, tall structures to be used as spaceports were added along the central canal."

HOLOTABLE

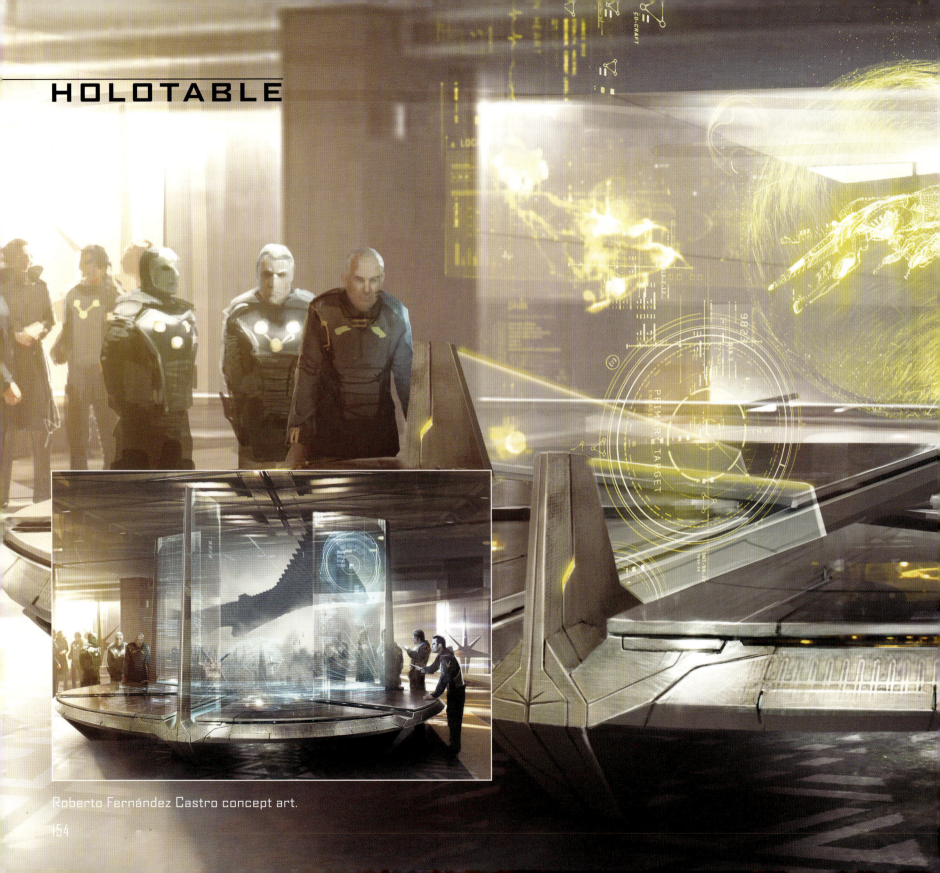

Roberto Fernández Castro concept art.

Concept Artist Roberto Fernández Castro designed the holotable at the center of the Nova Corps' headquarters. "I imagined it as a heavy piece of furniture, but also as an expensive jewel and a high-tech device," he says.

"I contrasted the heavy, solid exterior ring—beautifully decorated with Nova Corps emblems—with the central glass circle that reveals the complex holograph projector underneath."

CHAPTER FOUR: CORPS VALUES

155

NOVA PROCESSING CENTER

Roberto Fernández Castro concept art.

"I designed this room as a frame to present the Guardians in the movie," says Roberto Fernández Castro, who was tasked with imagining a police lineup in a sci-fi world. "In the image, Peter Quill is framed by the window, and the Nova Corps officers in the foreground can check his background and skills on the glass. The important element here is the character, so the background is a simple metal wall with height lines as in an actual police lineup."

NOVA CORPS

The Nova Corps has been patrolling the Marvel Comics universe since 1979, and its top brass is Nova Prime Centurion Irani Rael.

Concept Illustrator Jack Dudman wanted Rael's uniform to stand on its own yet still embrace the Corps' common language. "Her authority needed to come across in the uniform," he says. "These images were done to help sell the role to the actress Glenn Close."

Jack Dudman concept art.

CHAPTER FOUR: CORPS VALUES

'CORPSMAN' 'DENARIAN' 'MILLENNIAN'

'CENTURION' NOVA PRIME

Head of Visual Development Charlie Wen initiated the design process by creating a fully armored, helmeted Centurion. "Alex Byrne needed an entire workforce below that," Dudman continues. "We broke down Charlie's image, extending the style lines to evolve the look for the rest of the team."

Dudman worked out the Nova star insignias early as a basis for completing the uniforms. "The Centurians, Millennians, Denarians, and Corpsmen are all established ranks with long histories in the comics, so these were referenced heavily," he says.

Jack Dudman concept art.

NOVA CORPSMEN

"Above all, the Nova Corps needed to feel like an intergalactic, futuristic police force," Marvel Studios Head of Visual Development Charlie Wen says. "We went through a number of different thematic ideas—from Japanese mechanical influences to more present-day technology, and then going all the way toward futuristic and otherworldly tech."

Charlie Wen concept art.

"In the end, we found a nice blend of a formidable yet simplistic tech that felt streamlined and practical," Wen says. "There were some obvious design challenges to this in avoiding repetition of iconic looks, but it landed in its own space in the end."

Charlie Wen concept art.

Andy Park concept art.

CHAPTER FOUR: CORPS VALUES

"The Nova Corps are the ones tasked with initially arresting the Guardians, and then they team up with them at the very end of the movie to defeat Ronan as he tries to destroy planet Xandar," Co-Producer Jonathan Schwartz says.

Charlie Wen concept art.

Justin Sweet concept art. Jackson Sze concept art.

"In simplest terms, they're kind of like the space version of S.H.I.E.L.D.." Executive Producer Jeremy Latcham says. The Nova Corps decides to send the Guardians to the Kyln. "It's kind of like the bad side of the Nova Corps over there. John C. Reilly—who plays Dey—is really concerned about sending the Guardians there, because he's a really nice guy."

Justin Sweet concept art.

Anthony Francisco concept art.

Andy Park concept art.

Jackson Sze concept art.

CHAPTER FOUR: CORPS VALUES

165

Charlie Wen concept art.

Charlie Wen concept art. Charlie Wen concept art. Charlie Wen concept art.

Working from Wen's designs, other Visual Development artists further explored ideas for helmets. "The task required us to balance visor real estate with gold accents and helmet shapes," Concept Artist Jackson Sze says.

Jackson Sze concept art.

NOVA STARBLASTER

One of Charles Wood's favorite ships is the Starblaster. "It's based on an original concept from the Marvel magazines," Wood says.

"They have wings that flare out into a star," Visual Effects Supervisor Stephane Ceretti explains. "We looked at how some underwater creatures open up their tentacles. We looked at different references from the real world, from insects to fish, or at how fighter jets work."

Paul Catling concept art.

Concept Artist Paul Catling found the craft deceptively difficult to nail down. "In arrest mode, this one-man craft had to resemble the Nova Corps logo and be able to fold back the wings when flying about," he says. "It had to be in the Nova Corps' teal and gold colors. The cockpit area was most difficult to resolve. We didn't want a helicopter bubble of glass, but the pilot needed an unrestricted view of the city below. We added dazzle camouflage so the blend between paint and glass became imperceptible."

CHAPTER FOUR: CORPS VALUES

Paul Catling concept art.

Paul Catling concept art.

"The Starblaster opens from the front, so there couldn't be a complicated console," Catling says. "I painted the pilot using an articulated mechanical motion-capture device. The consoles fan up from the sides of the seat, which seemed like the only choice at the time."

Paul Catling concept art.

CHAPTER FOUR: CORPS VALUES

Phil Saunders concept art.

CHAPTER FOUR: CORPS VALUES

"I was taken with the idea that on attack, the enemy would see a flotilla of stars reminiscent of the Nova Corps logo descend upon them," says Concept Artist Phil Saunders, who worked on four ship concepts early in the pitch process. "I envisioned a stealthy dart-like ship that would unfold its wings to expose more of the propulsion surfaces for attack, making the star flare suddenly appear from a dead-on front view. Not to be too literal, I kept this 'star ship' to a six-pointed shape."

CHAPTER FIVE
PRISON BREAK

Pete Thompson concept art.

Star-Lord, Gamora, Rocket, and Groot are remanded to the remote, outer-space supermax called the Kyln, where Drax is also incarcerated.

"We had enormous sets in this movie," Director and Co-Writer James Gunn says. "The Kyln was composed of 350,000 pounds of steel."

The multilevel set was 38 feet tall. "The only thing that stopped us from going taller was the stage roof," Production Designer Charles Wood says. "It was a modular set, so we could change corridors. We designed something we could reuse many times in different configurations, which is what we did throughout the film."

The Kyln's configuration was based on a traditional prison layout, with a central watchtower and an octagonal area surrounded by cells.

"The space needed to work for the story and how the whole fight develops with all the characters—including Groot and Rocket—within the sequence," Wood says. "And James needed action beats, so we incorporated those into the design."

Concept Artist Pete Thompson worked closely with Wood to envision an iconic exterior. "We chose a big, heavy, abstract shape that looked threatening, with a great-looking silhouette," Thompson says. "It also had to tie in with the interior set. Everything about this ship was scrutinized down to the last detail—including size relative to the actual interior set, and how the Nova transporter docked into the side."

The set was three levels, and Visual Effects extended it about thirty more.

"For a few shots, we had to rebuild the entire set as a CG asset because the camera moves were too extreme to be shot with normal plates," Visual Effects Supervisor Stephane Ceretti says. "But having so much of that set built was great reference for us."

THE KYLN
M2QH 119919142+018511

For the impound area, Pete Thompson took inspiration from modern, vertical car parks. "I gave it a junkier feel that looked dirty and slightly chaotic," he says. "We needed to show various vehicles and spacecraft—including the Milano—from around the galaxy, all impounded after arrest."

Pete Thompson concept art.

CHAPTER FIVE: PRISON BREAK

"Some of the initial designs show the progression of what we were looking for design-wise," Thompson says. "Once the concept art was approved, we moved into 3-D, and the renders were sent back to me for a final paint-over and lighting pass. Once that was completed, I did some final set-extension paintings to show the ceiling area and upper decks that would be greenscreen."

Pete Thompson concept art.

CHAPTER FIVE: PRISON BREAK

Pete Thompson concept art.

Pete Thompson concept art.

CHAPTER FIVE: PRISON BREAK

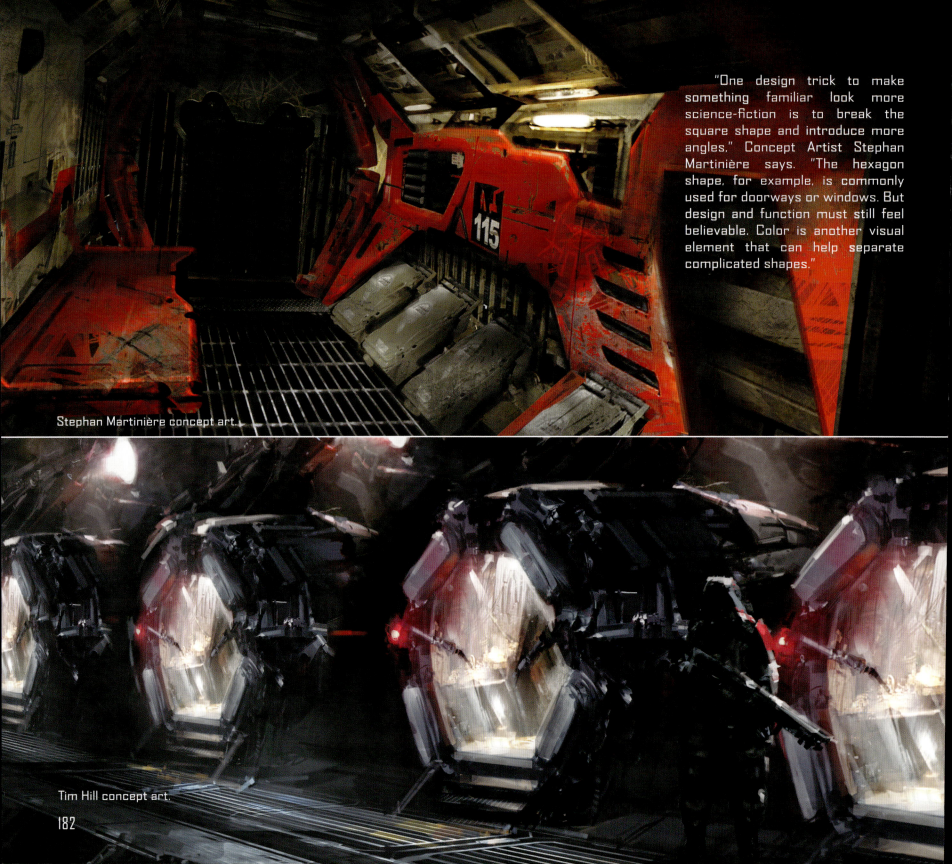

"One design trick to make something familiar look more science-fiction is to break the square shape and introduce more angles," Concept Artist Stephan Martinière says. "The hexagon shape, for example, is commonly used for doorways or windows. But design and function must still feel believable. Color is another visual element that can help separate complicated shapes."

Stephan Martinière concept art.

Tim Hill concept art.

CHAPTER FIVE: PRISON BREAK

Pete Thompson concept art.

Pete Thompson concept art.

PRISONERS

"I was thinking about the archetypes I'd seen in prison shows," Concept Artist Josh Herman says. "I wanted this guy to be muscular and intimidating. He uses his size to push people around and get what he wants, which is an animalistic way to act, so I wanted to include some animal traits in his head shape while keeping him humanoid."

Concept art by Josh Herman & Jack Dudman.

Colin Shulver/SMUFX concept art.

Colin Shulver/SMUFX concept art.

Concept art by Colin Shulver & David White/SMUFX.

Concept art by Colin Shulver & David White/SMUFX.

184

CHAPTER FIVE: PRISON BREAK

Josh Herman concept art.

Ryan Meinerding concept art.

Charlie Wen concept art.

Anthony Francisco concept art.

"I decided to design a restraint collar on this guy to show that he's so dangerous he always has to be shackled," Concept Artist Jerad Marantz says. "I love the challenge of bringing these bizarre comic-book characters to life."

Jerad Marantz concept art.

185

Pete Thompson keyframe.

"I think everyone in the production crew would agree with me that the Kyln was the most impressive set of the whole movie," Thompson says. "We spent month after month concepting this location until it was perfect in every way."

CHAPTER FIVE: PRISON BREAK

Anthony Francisco keyframe.

"I had to find a simple composition so that I could showcase the different types of aliens and humans interacting with one another," says Concept Artist Anthony Francisco, who found showing a variety of aliens in a single image a fun task to explore.

CHAPTER FIVE: PRISON BREAK

189

"The goal here was to have the different alien species look natural together." Concept Artist Rodney Fuentebella says. "I wanted to convey how an alien prison would feel—a sense of ordered chaos, anxiety, and frustration. Some would gather to pass the time leisurely, and others by picking fights or whatever they can do in a contained environment. I wanted to make sure that no alien race appears superior to another. How the individual copes with prison determines their fate. These scenes are fun to paint because there can be a lot of moments playing out at the same time, which the audience may or may not notice."

Rodney Fuentebella keyframe.

CHAPTER FIVE: PRISON BREAK

DRAX

Colin Shulvers sculpting Drax's prosthetics.

Eighty-five percent of Drax's torso is covered in red keloid scarring, on display whenever he's on screen. "Every time a character wears the prosthetics, the pieces have to be trashed and a new set applied the next day, and David Bautista was going to work nearly every day," Special Make-Up Effects Designer David White says of the challenges faced by his team.

Justin Sweet concept art.

"Drax's prosthetic silicone covering also had to look a little translucent, like real scarred skin, so I sculpted the prosthetics on a life cast of David," White continues. "Then we cut out a practical pattern for application, floated the sections off, flattened them out, and molded them. This meant we could cast the prosthetics individually with a very particular Drax red color and a second layer of gray Drax base, which is his real Drax skin tone. This process meant the painting of the Drax prosthetics was fast and accurate every time, and the prosthetics were thin and flexible enough to be applied to David Bautista every day for the duration of the shoot."

Justin Sweet concept art.

CHAPTER FIVE: PRISON BREAK

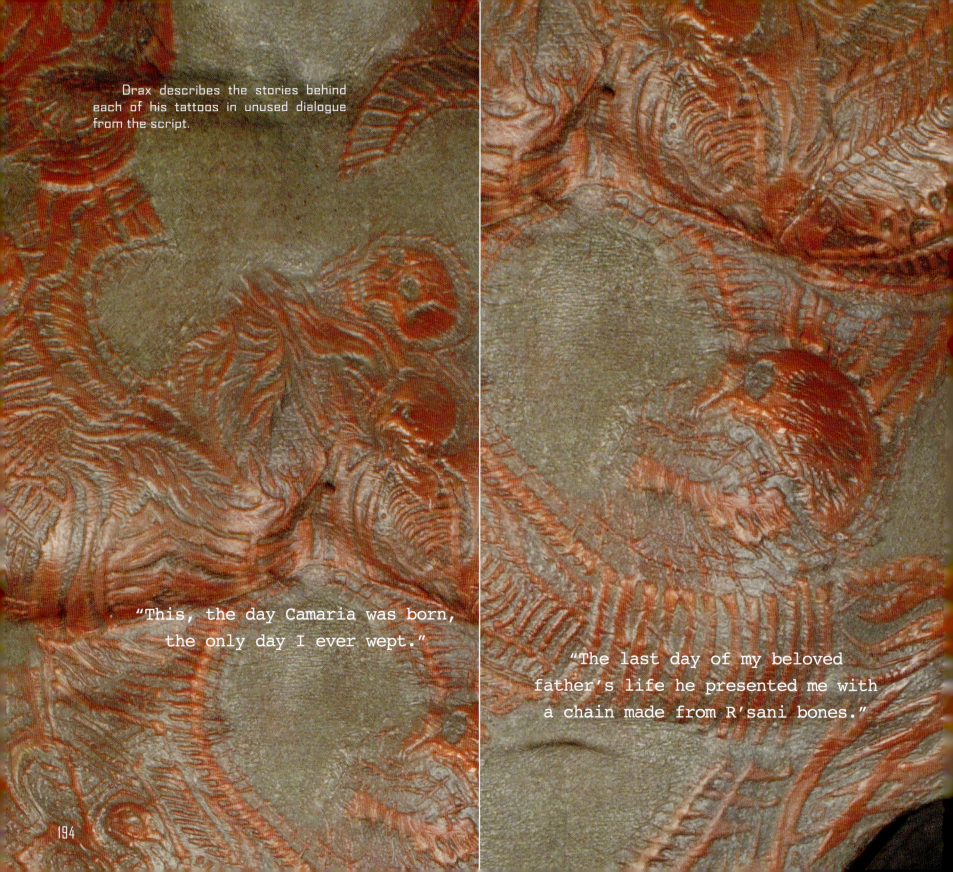

Drax describes the stories behind each of his tattoos in unused dialogue from the script.

"This, the day Camaria was born, the only day I ever wept."

"The last day of my beloved father's life he presented me with a chain made from R'sani bones."

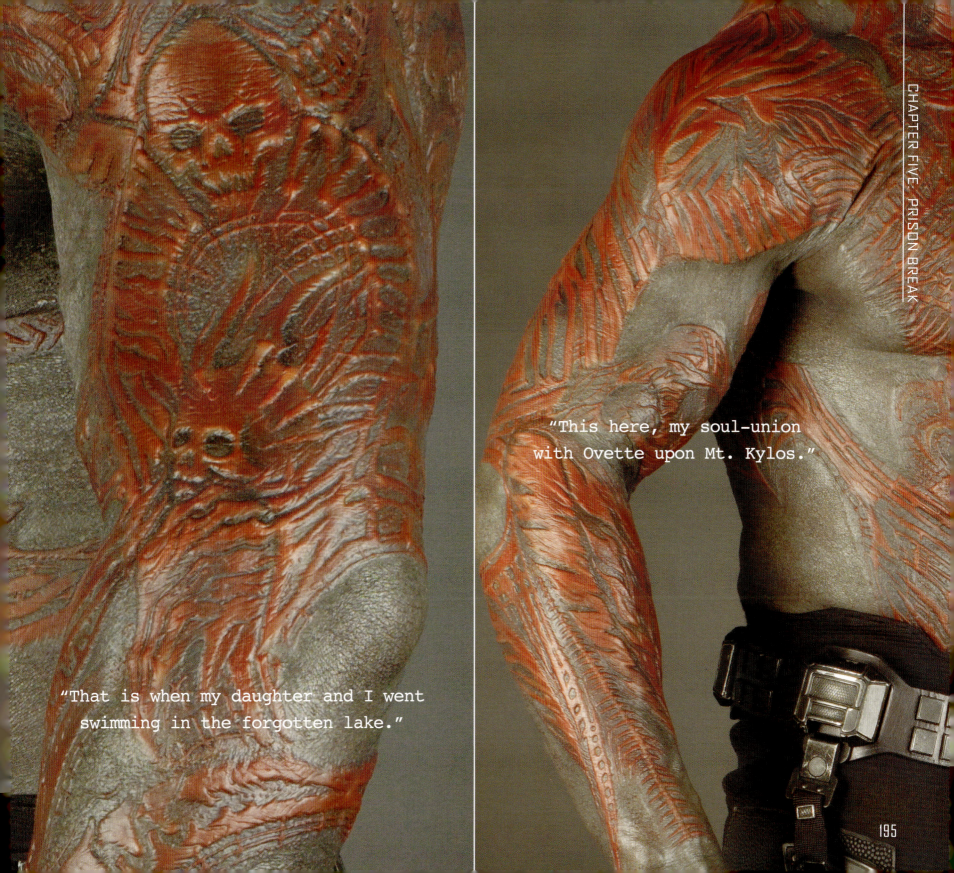

"That is when my daughter and I went swimming in the forgotten lake."

"This here, my soul-union with Ovette upon Mt. Kylos."

CHAPTER FIVE: PRISON BREAK

"All the tattoos on Drax's body meant something important about his family—like about his daughter and wife and father," Concept Artist Justin Sweet says. "But he needed to look scary, too—so even though the moments are reflective, they look kind of demonic. It's intended to be from his culture."

Justin Sweet concept art.

"The character of Drax is really complex," Executive Producer Jeremy Latcham says. "What you have is a guy who is pure vengeance; all he wants to do is get vengeance on the people that murdered his wife, murdered his daughter, ruined his life, and took everything away from him. And so you meet him and you see this big, hulking guy covered in tattoos, covered in scarification, and he looks like a menace and you think, 'This guy is just a bruiser.'"

Justin Sweet concept art.

Andy Park concept art.

CHAPTER FIVE: PRISON BREAK

"Over the course of the film, you kind of peel back the layers and what you realize is Drax is not just a bruiser," Latcham says. "He is a deeply sorrowful, regretful man who wants to make amends for the awful things that have happened in his life and that took everything from him."

Andy Park concept art.

Charlie Wen concept art.

"When we first meet Drax, he is serving jail time due to killing some of Ronan's minions," Executive Producer and Marvel Studios Co-President Louis D'Esposito says. "He learns that Gamora is working with Ronan and decides to kill her, but is ultimately dissuaded by Peter Quill. When Peter, Rocket, Groot, and Gamora decide to break out of prison, Drax joins them and helps them escape while preparing for his revenge against Ronan. When Drax finally has the opportunity to confront Ronan, he risks the lives of the other Guardians and causes them to lose possession of the Orb."

Justin Sweet concept art.

CHAPTER FIVE: PRISON BREAK

"In the comic books, Drax has very distinct tattoos, so I tried to come up with various ways we could achieve that look without simply having a literal tattoo of red swirls," Concept Artist Andy Park says. "I tried scarification, and the red being light body armor worn by the warriors of his race."

Andy Park concept art.

"The lack of full coverage could be a mark of the skill and ferocity of that warrior, a method of intimidation. I even played with the idea that Drax was genetically and technologically altered to be the finest warrior. Justin Sweet eventually came up with his final, amazing look."

CHAPTER FIVE: PRISON BREAK

"Drawing heavily muscled Drax reminded me of being a kid and loving comic books and drawing super heroes," Sweet says. "It was fun to go back and inhabit that space."

Justin Sweet concept art.

"Director James Gunn had specific ideas about Drax standing up to the Necrocrafts," Sweet says. "He really wanted Drax to be looking back so the viewer could see his profile. He sent a storyboard for the position of Drax."

Justin Sweet keyframe.

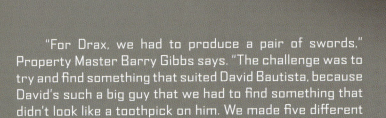

"For Drax, we had to produce a pair of swords," Property Master Barry Gibbs says. "The challenge was to try and find something that suited David Bautista, because David's such a big guy that we had to find something that didn't look like a toothpick on him. We made five different scales for him, eventually landing on something that was about 19 inches long. It was governed by the length of his leg, so we had to produce scabbards which fit into the boots and pop those on."

CHAPTER FIVE: PRISON BREAK

KYLN GUARDS

"The guards were originally their own private security force, but they evolved into becoming an offshoot of the Nova Corps left to their own devices for too long," Concept Illustrator Jack Dudman says. "The brief was that these were essentially thugs. They had Nova kits of their own—but broken down, unwashed, possibly caked with dirt, blood, and sweat. You didn't want to meet these guys."

Jack Dudman concept art.

Under arm connections

Top

CHAPTER FIVE: PRISON BREAK

Christopher Caldow concept art.

Concept Artist Christopher Caldow sketched the Nova taser rod and Kyln bazooka, then modeled the prop geometry in 3-D before digitally painting over his 3-D renders. "Once I'd refined these ideas and added shading, color, and texture, I passed my designs to Set Decorator Richard Roberts," he says.

KYLN BAZOOKA
PRISON GUARD

"Richard pushed me artistically further and further in order to get the best possible result, and Charles Wood was very keen on detail," Caldow says. "By the end of the design process, they had fully realized prop concept designs, and on it went to Barry Gibbs and his team to turn the ideas into reality."

Christopher Caldow concept art.

KYLN HOVERBOTS

Paul Catling concept art.

Concept Artist Paul Catling immediately noticed that the Kyln Hoverbot's look was dictated by function. "It hovers and fires lots of bullets," he says. "I worked up three concepts, and James Gunn liked one early in the process, so I modeled in 3-D. Because it has a lot of moving parts, it is much easier to understand in 3-D—to determine whether parts intersect with each other and whether it would actually work in the real world."

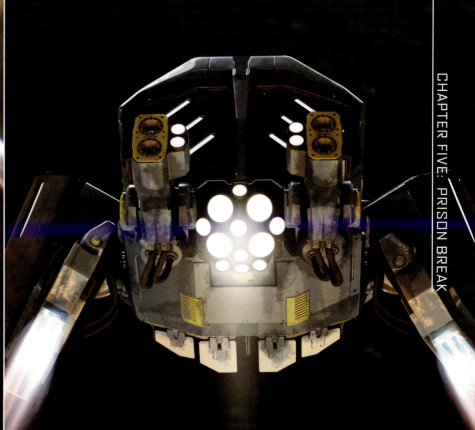

CHAPTER FIVE: PRISON BREAK

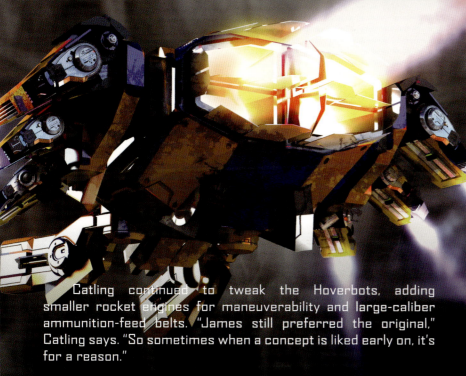

Catling continued to tweak the Hoverbots, adding smaller rocket engines for maneuverability and large-caliber ammunition-feed belts. "James still preferred the original," Catling says. "So sometimes when a concept is liked early on, it's for a reason."

Paul Catling concept art.

KYLN ESCAPE
STORYBOARDS BY DAVID KRENTZ

To escape the Kyln, the group must act as a team for the first time—and put their trust in Rocket. "There was so much going on in this sequence," Storyboard Artist David Krentz says.

"I loved that only Rocket knew what his plan was, and he kept it to himself. Everything goes haywire, but he still manages to make it look like he knew what he was doing the whole time!"

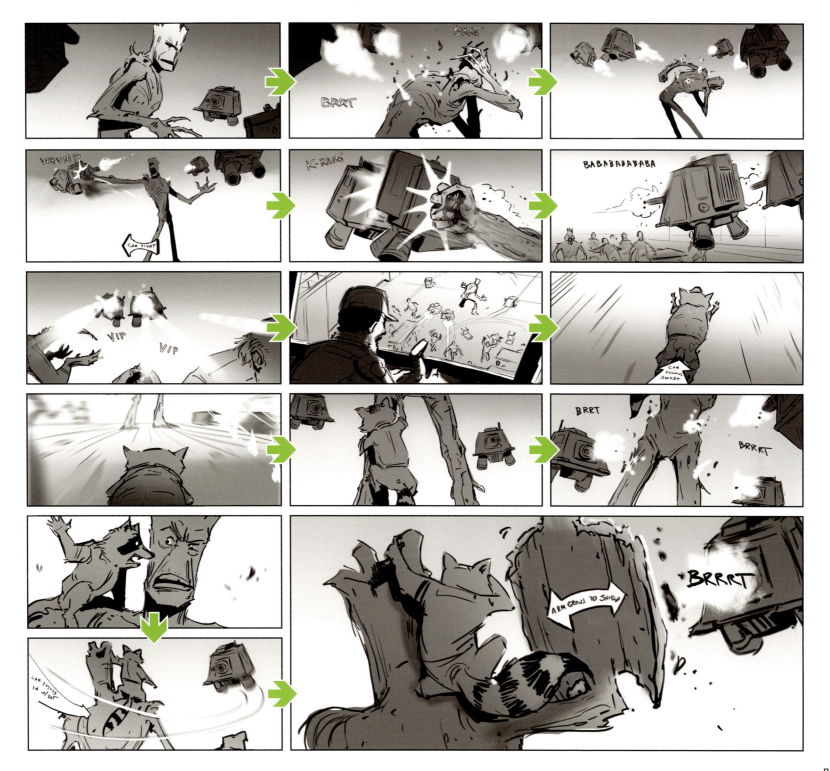

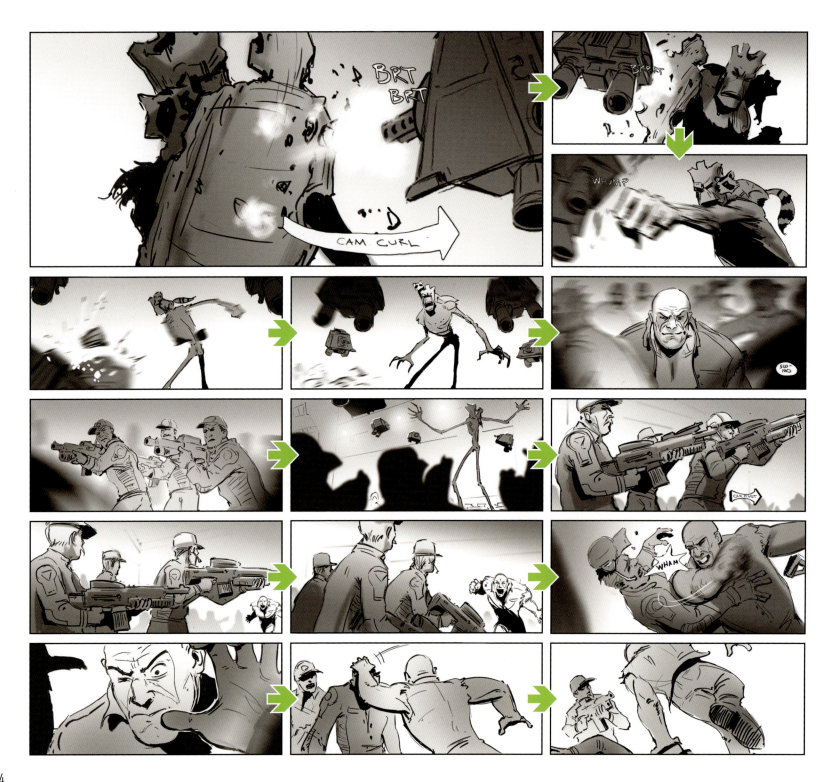

"Since there was so much motion and confusion going on, the camera was constantly moving," Krentz says. "James loved to have shots where the camera curled/rotated/pivoted in one direction while the actions of the characters spun the other way. That kind of movement was a perfect device to get inside the character's heads as they struggle to keep control of the spiraling situation. When I board, especially in my first rough pass, I draw as fast as I can so I can really get lost in the moment. And just like when I was a little kid, I get so excited I make sound effects when I draw. That's actually when I know the scene is working!"

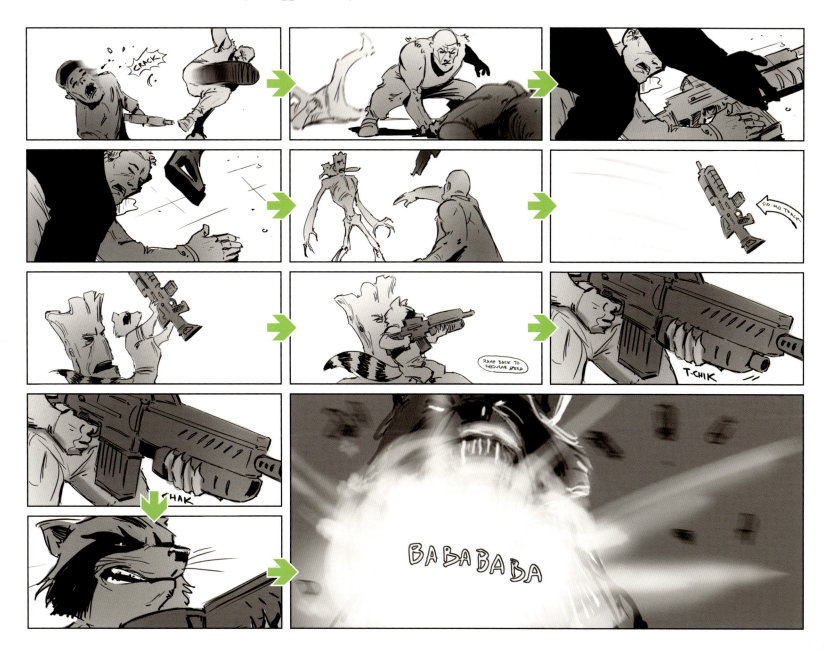

"This was really fun to paint," Concept Artist Jackson Sze says. "I enjoy the friendship these two found in each other. When all else fails, they will always have each other's backs."

Jackson Sze keyframe.

CHAPTER FIVE: PRISON BREAK

CHAPTER FIVE: PRISON BREAK

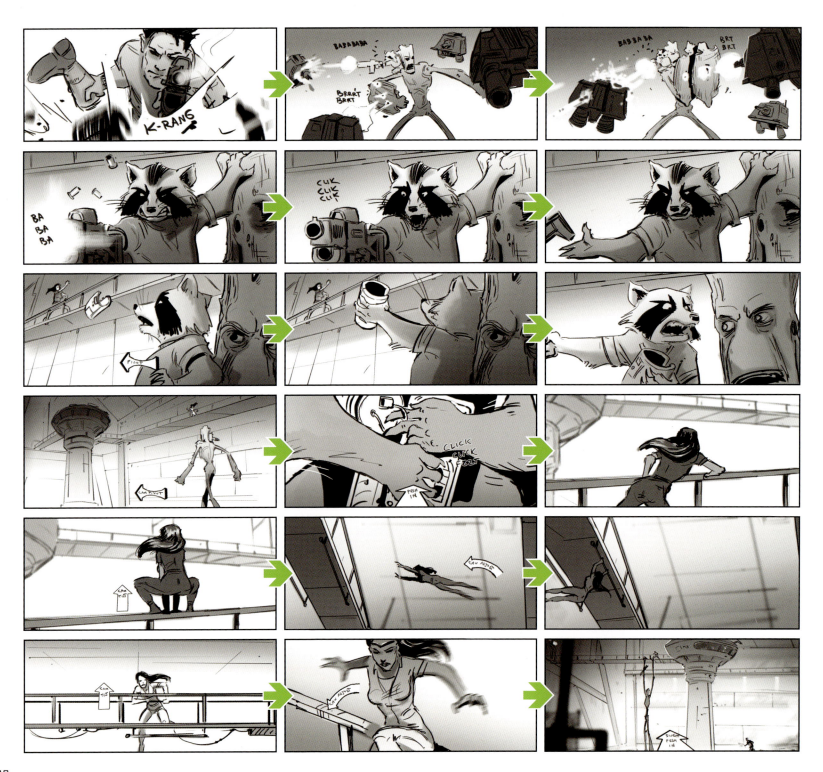

CHAPTER FIVE: PRISON BREAK

  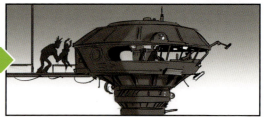

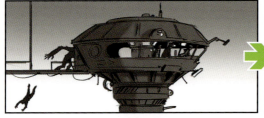  

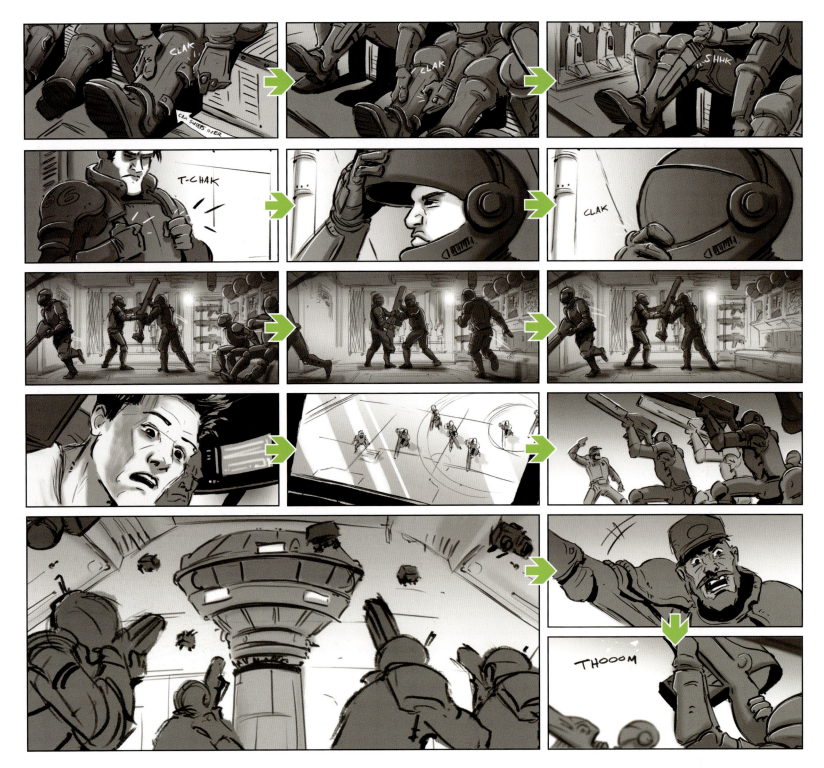

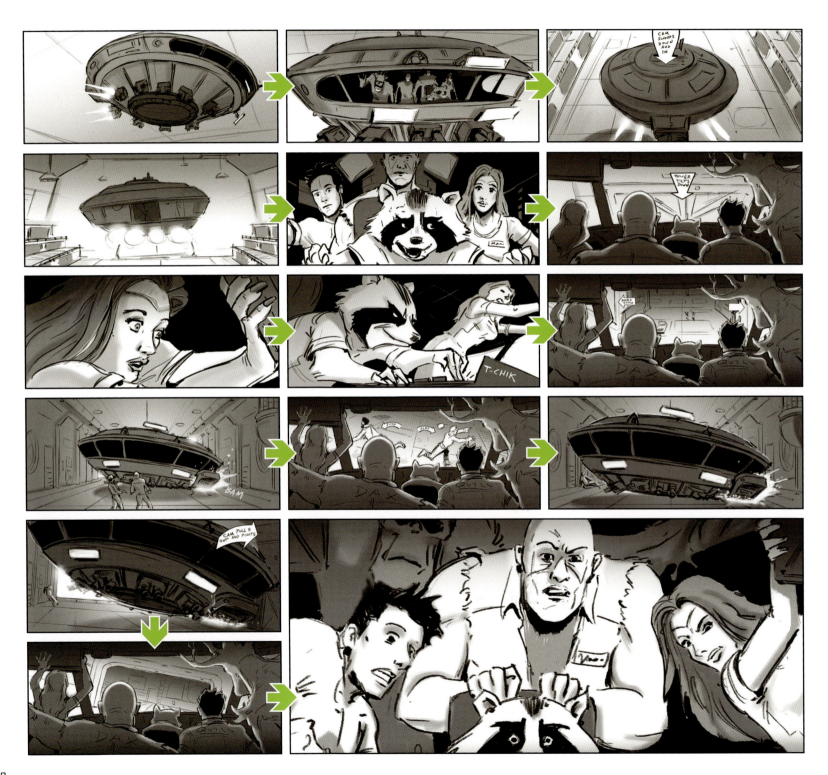

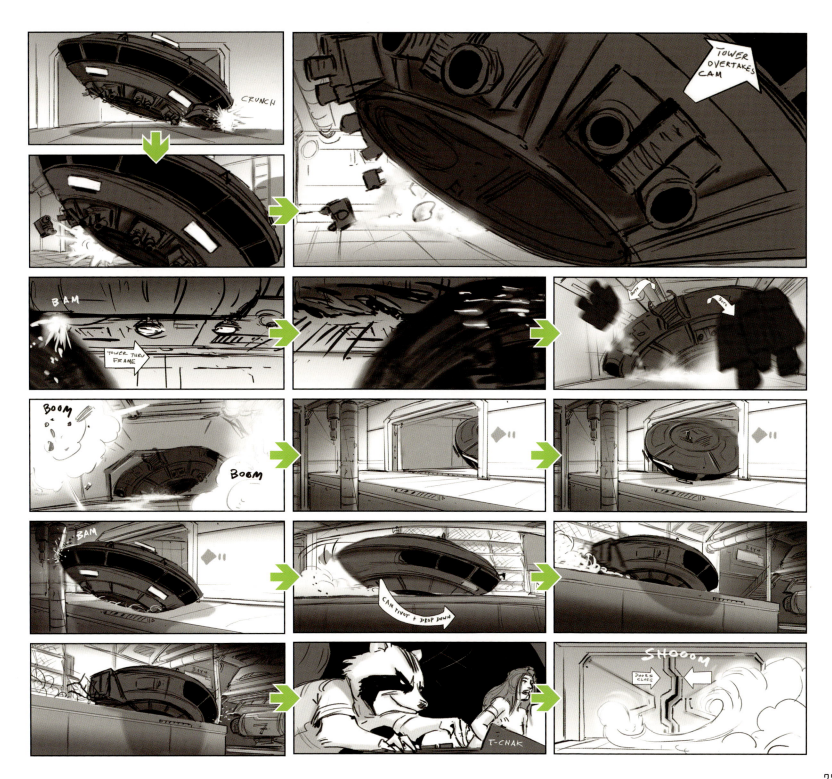

CHAPTER SIX
KNOWHERE TO RUN

Framestore VFX still.

Peter Quill and his fragile alliance of unlikely loners are united on at least one front: avoiding the law's reach. Once again in possession of the Orb, the team heads to a mining world and outpost on the edge of the galaxy called Knowhere, home to the mysterious Collector.

Knowhere is the giant severed head of a member of the race of higher cosmic beings called the Celestials. It's part metal and part organic, and it orbits a black hole eating a sun.

"That was probably the most abstract thing we did in the film, and we did many concepts of what this entity would look like," Production Designer Charles Wood says. "Some of them were so mad, you could have come up with that sort of thing in the '60s. It was really challenging."

A section of a Knowhere street was built at Longcross Film Studios in London. Visual Effects took it from there.

"The walls of Knowhere are made of bones," Visual Effects Supervisor Stephane Ceretti says. "So for reference, we looked at what bones and skulls look like. Director and Co-Writer James Gunn wanted to feel the flesh that was still stuck to the bone inside the Celestial's head. And it's got a huge spine in the back of the head, so we had to get the spine made. Then there's all this mining equipment attached to the spine—it was a huge, huge build."

KNOWHERE
M3RD 17H17211+2121224

For his work on *Guardians*, Concept Artist Kevin Jenkins tried to evoke the colorful '70's book-jacket artwork that influenced him as a kid. "I was deliberately trying to show the scale of the giant Celestial head, but show it in such a way that you had to look twice to understand it," he says. "Just doing two eyes and a mouth would have been too obvious, too on-the-nose."

Kevin Jenkins concept art.

"Knowhere has a fair bit of comic-book folklore attached to it," Concept Artist Pete Thompson says. "So I researched before diving in. We came up with something that felt industrial and otherworldly and ethereal."

Pete Thompson concept art.

CHAPTER SIX: KNOWHERE TO RUN

The alien species of *Guardians* range in skin tone from deep blue to bubblegum pink. "Color is something I work very instinctively with," Costume Designer Alexandra Byrne says. "I was really struggling with some of the fittings and wondering why it was so difficult. Then I realized one of my main tools had been taken away, because I usually work with natural skin tones. Once I realized that, I quit fighting it and said, 'This is a thing, this is a design factor' and learned how to make it work."

Jackson Sze keyframe.

Kevin Jenkins concept art.

Pete Thompson concept art.

Thompson envisioned a vast city of buildings, bridges, bustling streets, and markets inside the Celestial head. "We wanted to give the impression that people had lived in this thing for centuries, that it had layers of history with older buildings next to newer buildings," he says.

BOOT OF JEMIAH

"This aliens-and-humans group shot showing the nightlife in one of the taverns of Knowhere started off with just the drinking buddies in the foreground, then expanded to include more of the bar and the nightclub," Concept Artist Anthony Francisco says.

Anthony Francisco keyframe.

Justin Sweet keyframe.

CHAPTER SIX: KNOWHERE TO RUN

Rodney Fuentebella keyframe.

239

Concept art by Jack Dudman & Warren Holder.

"These five versions of yellow pool miners had elements that could be mixed and matched over many background artists to create a larger number of looks, especially once makeup and prosthetics were added," Concept Illustrator Jack Dudman says.

Jack Dudman concept art.

Costume Design concept art.

Magdalena Kusowska concept art.

CHAPTER SIX: KNOWHERE TO RUN

241

FEMALIENS

The women of the Boot of Jemiah are as strange as the world in which they live. "They are supposed to convey otherworldliness," Concept Artist Magdalena Kusowska says. "They are sexy, dangerously odd. They catch your attention but throw you, as well."

Magdalena Kusowska concept art.

Jack Dudman concept art.

Jack Dudman concept art.

Jack Dudman concept art.

Jack Dudman concept art.

"Alex had fantastic mood boards that clearly communicated the design direction," Kusowska says. "The alien girls have their own clothing language, conveyed through an unusual, inventive wardrobe. The idea for the jewelry came from random collections of coins and medallions that together show a combination of rusty and bluish colors wrapped around wrists, ankles, and chest."

Magdalena Kusowska concept art.

Jack Dudman concept art.

Magdalena Kusowska concept art.

CHAPTER SIX: KNOWHERE TO RUN

"The bar girls were a great set of characters to go big on with the colors," Jack Dudman says. "I also viewed it as a way to get some more lines from the comics in. Usually the background comic-book characters are drawn as figures with basic colorful outfits almost sprayed on, and this I thought would be a nice, logical place to nod to that."

Jack Dudman concept art.

Magdalena Kusowska concept art.

CHAPTER SIX: KNOWHERE TO RUN

Alexandra Byrne referenced contemporary fashion blogs with an eye to the women who had been cast. "We became experts in latex," she says. "And we worked closely with Makeup because the hair is part of the silhouette."

Magdalena Kusowska concept art.

Drax, Rocket, and Groot head to a gaming track at the center of the Boot of Jemiah. "The table is a dangerous object, made of sharp metal, full of traps that the gamblers can control from the sides to stop the small creatures and try to win the game," Concept Artist Roberto Fernández Castro says. "In the design process, we had to think about the rules of this mad game to find a believable and successful design."

Roberto Fernández Castro concept art.

CHAPTER SIX: KNOWHERE TO RUN

247

ORLONI & F'SAKI

"The keyword we got for this creature was 'rat-like,'" Concept Artist Andrew Kim says of the Orlani. "For the F'sakis, the keywords were 'frog- and bulldog-like.' The Orlanis would race, I assume, like dogs, and the F'sakis are supposed to chase the Orlanis and actually eat them. So expect to see some graphic scenes when these guys are shown on the screen!"

Andrew Kim concept art.

Andrew Kim concept art.

Anthony Francisco concept art.

CHAPTER SIX: KNOWHERE TO RUN

Anthony Francisco immediately thought of killer racing bullfrogs for the F'saki. "Frogs already look alien," he says. "I just had to make them aggressive. I imagined that in millions of years, frogs might evolve, developing teeth and more streamlined bodies."

Anthony Francisco concept art.

249

COLLECTOR'S MUSEUM/LAB

The galaxy's most comprehensive assemblage of artifacts, both animate and inanimate, is on Knowhere—curated by the enigmatic Collector and his assistant, Carina.

"No two display boxes have the same stuff in them," Stephane Ceretti says. "We had cases and boxes and set dressing on that set—but we needed to make the space much, much bigger. And all this required a proper CG build, because we blow up the place at the end. We had to build all those things. It was a pretty big job."

Roberto Fernández Castro concept art.

"The Collector's lab shows this collection of unworldly, exotic, eclectic goods in a warehouse," Property Master Barry Gibbs says. "The Collector has gathered up Terrans or humanoids, aliens, exquisite plants, exquisite ornaments from anywhere in the universe or universes. And you'll see that we've created things from other Marvel worlds too." Watch carefully.

Roberto Fernández Castro concept art.

CHAPTER SIX: KNOWHERE TO RUN

Concept Artist Richard Anderson used the Collector's body language to convey his protectiveness of his vast collection. "I was also trying to portray that everything in the universe has its own sense of scale," he says. "So if you get an item from one planet, it might be a plant cell and still be as big as the Titanic in our eyes."

Roberto Fernández Castro concept art.

Richard Anderson concept art.

Kevin Jenkins concept art.

Richard Anderson concept art.

THE COLLECTION

"What do you need, mortal? I have many things in my collection."
—The Collector, *Avengers Assemble* (2012) #8

Taneleer Tivan's collection of both living and inanimate objects is the most comprehensive assortment of artifacts in the known galaxy. You never know what you might find in his display cases.

Rocket discovers Cosmo, the labrador who developed psychic abilities after a Soviet space experiment launched him into orbit. But behind Rocket stares an imprisoned Chitauri. The aliens invaded Earth on behalf of Thanos, working with Loki, in *Marvel's The Avengers*.

Behind Carina, a Dark Elf sits in captivity. Dark Elves were believed extinct until they rose to fight Asgard in Marvel's *Thor: The Dark World*. Marvel fans might recognize a cosmic cocoon of great significance in the comics.

And an assortment of many more Marvel characters await in Tivan's collection for the eagle-eyed fan…

Cosmo concept art by Jack Dudman. LEFT: Cosmo, as seen in *Guardians of the Galaxy (2008) #2*.

The Dark Elves, as seen in Marvel's *Thor: The Dark World*.

Cosmic cocoon, as seen in *Marvel Premiere (1972) #1*.

The Chitauri, as seen in *Marvel's The Avengers*.

THE POWER STONE

"Before creation itself...there were six singularities. Then the universe exploded into existence, and the remnants of these systems were forged into concentrated ingots: Infinity Stones."
    –Taneleer Tivan

Marvel's *Guardians of the Galaxy*

THE COLLECTOR

The Collector has a long history in Marvel Comics. Concept Artist Jackson Sze started with that reference, but the character evolved with the casting. "Different body types lend themselves to different character design," Sze says. "Throughout them, the sense of opulence and power needs to come through. A simpler design had been approved before Benicio Del Toro was cast. He was eager to play up the flamboyant aspect of the Collector, so a new design was created. The furs and cape gave him more to play with on set. His makeup also helped transform him more completely into a powerful humanoid alien."

Jackson Sze concept art.

Anthony Francisco envisioned a macho version of the Collector. "I tried making him a thrill-of-the-kill kind of guy who would kill elephants and wrestle with alligators, but it would be aliens instead of animals," he says.

Anthony Francisco concept art.

CHAPTER SIX: KNOWHERE TO RUN

"He's willing to buy the Orb for quite a bit of money," Executive Producer Jeremy Latcham says. "But the Collector is this very compromised guy. You know, do you really want to trust a guy that has all kinds of people living in cages in his place? But he knows what he's talking about. He's kind of got this seductive charm about him. He's kind of creepy. It's pretty cool."

Jackson Sze concept art.

Jackson Sze concept art.

CHAPTER SIX: KNOWHERE TO RUN

CARINA

Magdalena Kusowska concept art.

"Carina was a fun character to help design," Concept Artist Andy Park says. "Her general face was first designed by Anthony Francisco. She is a servant of the Collector, and I wanted to create a 'cute and subservient' look that is a result of her predicament more than a personal sense of fashion."

Andy Park concept art.

Andy Park concept art.

Anthony Francisco concept art.

CHAPTER SIX: KNOWHERE TO RUN

Andy Park depicted the moment when Carina fights back. "She is tired of her trapped existence and desperately seeking an out. It's a sad and unfortunate moment when she discovers the power of the stone."

Andy Park keyframe.

CHAPTER SIX : KNOWHERE TO RUN

Pete Thompson grounded Knowhere's spacepod garage with a familiar industrial look. "The crew came up with a really small set," Thompson says. "The main pod on the left was constructed in parts from a 3-D printer and assembled on set. The remainder of the set was greenscreen, so it was my job to paint in the bits that were missing on set. For example, the part of the floor that drops down, and the rows and rows of pods parked in the garage in the distance."

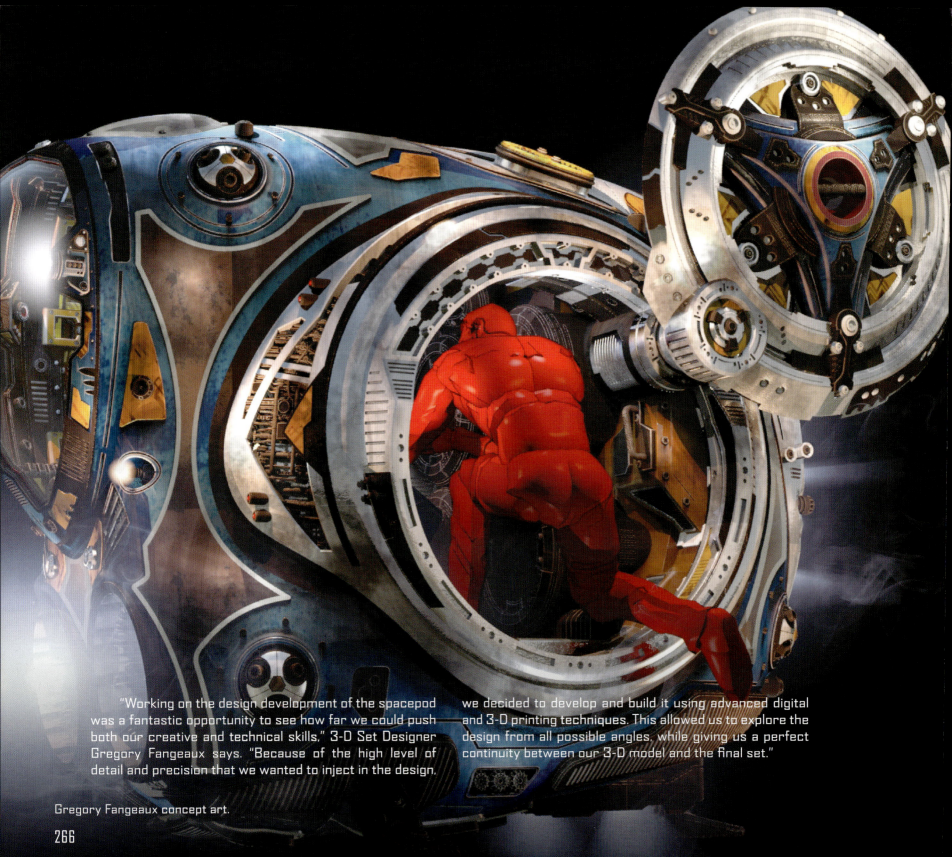

"Working on the design development of the spacepod was a fantastic opportunity to see how far we could push both our creative and technical skills," 3-D Set Designer Gregory Fangeaux says. "Because of the high level of detail and precision that we wanted to inject in the design, we decided to develop and build it using advanced digital and 3-D printing techniques. This allowed us to explore the design from all possible angles, while giving us a perfect continuity between our 3-D model and the final set."

Gregory Fangeaux concept art.

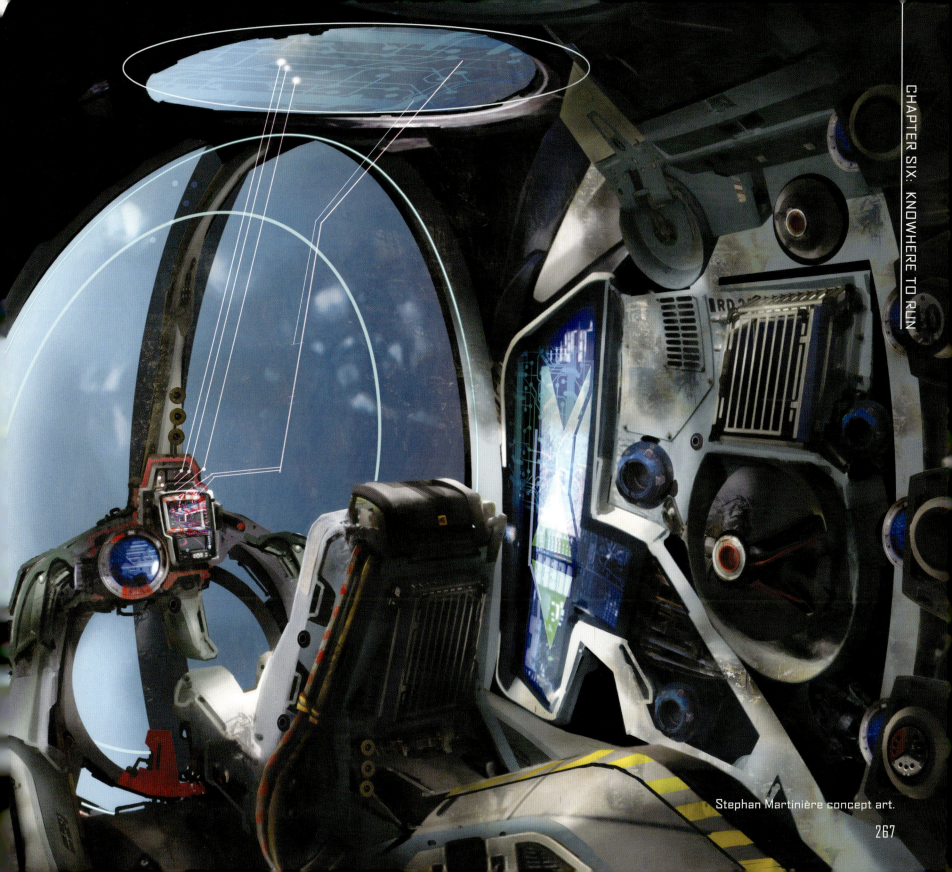

Stephan Martinière concept art.

CHAPTER SIX: KNOWHERE TO RUN

"Establishing a good digital workflow early on is extremely important," Fangeaux says. "Even at an early stage of the design, the 3-D model of the spacepod could be passed on to the pre-viz team so we could see it in action at the heart of the story, while having the same model in the hands of the SFX crew so they could build the most impressive inner steel structure and mechanisms for the doors and all moving parts. This is what this schematic visual is about, an assembly and requirements guide for all the people involved in the making of this amazing vehicle."

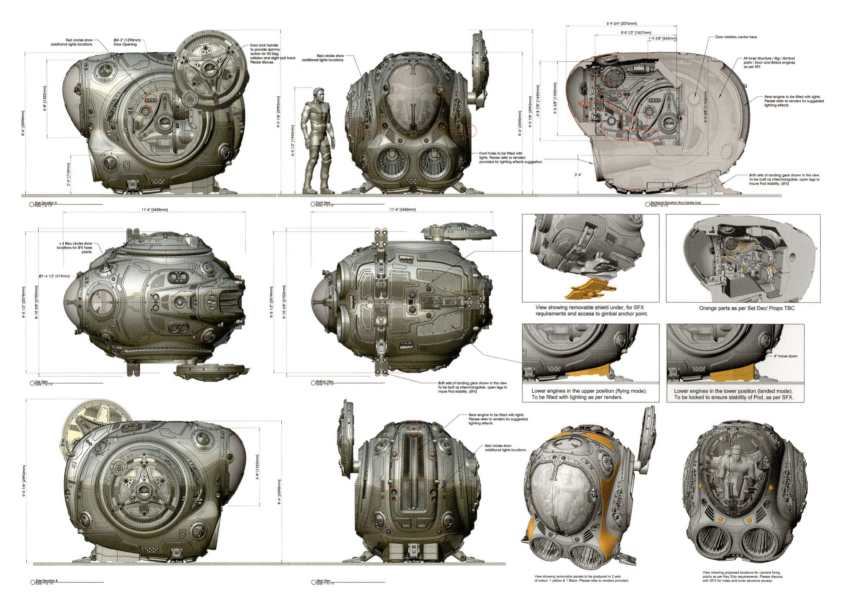

Gregory Fangeaux concept art.

○ Sectional Views Showing Positioning of Bike & Pilot
Scale: NTS

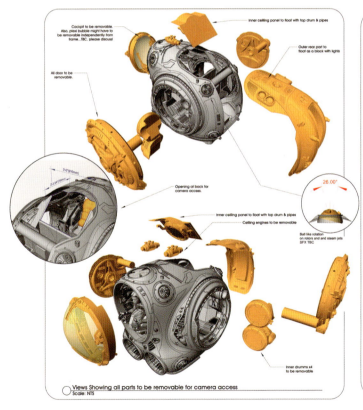

○ Views Showing all parts to be removable for camera access
Scale: NTS

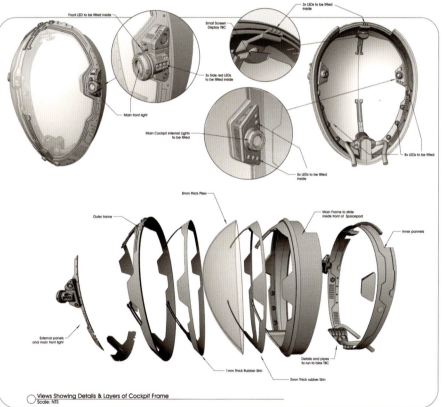

○ Views Showing Details & Layers of Cockpit Frame
Scale: NTS

CHAPTER SIX: KNOWHERE TO RUN

In a move that cements his role as hero, Quill rescues Gamora after she is thrown from her destroyed ship. "She is floating weightlessly while Quill demonstrates self-sacrifice and love by giving his own oxygen to her," Charlie Wen says. "All the debris serenely floating around them contrasts with the emotion of the moment and Quill's frantic effort to save Gamora. The light slowly engulfs them when Yondu's calvary arrives."

Charlie Wen keyframe.

CHAPTER SIX: KNOWHERE TO RUN

Charlie Wen keyframe.

CHAPTER SIX: KNOWHERE TO RUN

273

CHAPTER SEVEN
FAMILY REUNION

Tim Hill concept art.

Yondu Udonta plucks Star-Lord and Gamora out of the suffocating cosmos and drops them back into the land of the living.

But Udonta's Ravagers are scoundrels operating on society's fringes. Peter Quill, for all his grandiose notions of being a lord among the stars, was raised by a band of space pirates. He aspires to be more than an outlaw, but it's his rough-and-tumble adoptive family that saves him and his team in the end. Quill has learned he can form new bonds, establish a new family of his choosing, and become more than he was—but not without acknowledging his past.

"Yondu is not a bad guy," Executive Producer Jeremy Latcham says. "He's a Ravager, and they're basically galactic con men and vagabonds. Yondu is Quill's father figure, just not a very good one. Quill's swagger and some of his charming qualities come from Yondu. When you see the two of them together on screen, you realize that there's definitely a kinship between them."

Every pirate needs a ship, and Yondu has the Ecclector—a rugged, badly maintained, dangerous-looking craft. "Over the years, it's been retrofitted and patched up with all kinds of parts from other ships," Concept Artist Tim Hill says. "The challenge here was to create a ship that still had a strong identity, not to create a flying junkyard! I based the whole design on a submarine under construction."

RAVAGER FIGHTERS

Concept Artist Roberto Fernández Castro created orthographic views of the Ravager Fighter and Rocket's Warbird in high resolution, making them perfect guides for producing final 3-D models. "In those drawings, it is possible to see the different metal textures, the shut lines, or the rivets joining different metal plates," Castro says.

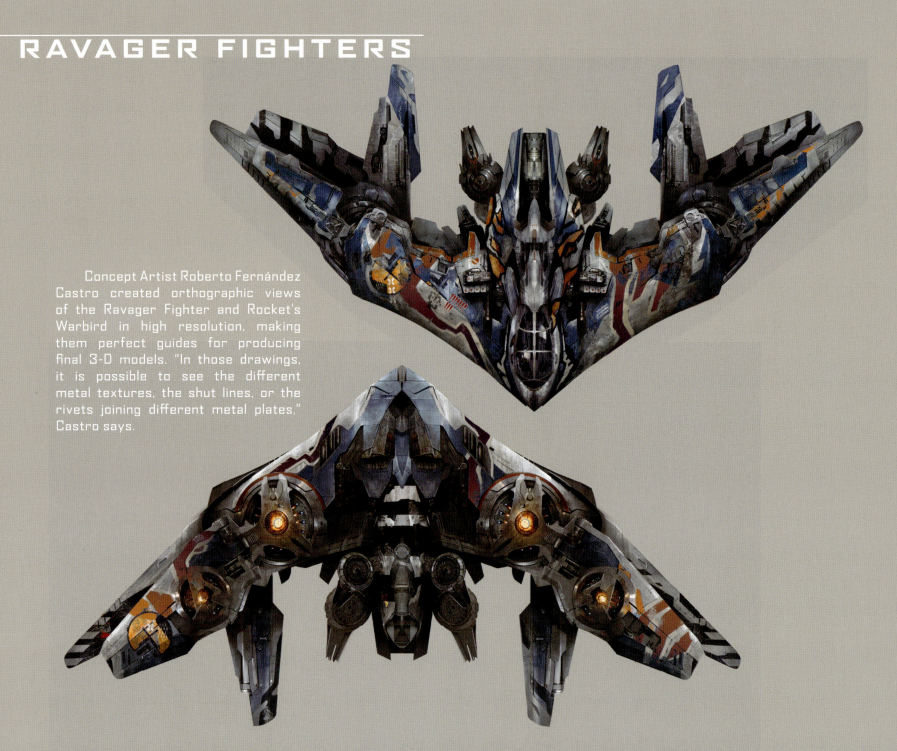

Roberto Fernández Castro concept art/Pete Thompson graphics.

As with Star-Lord and the Milano, Castro infused Rocket's Warbird with a bit of the character's personality. "I decided to do a slightly smaller fighter than the Milano, but equipped with two massive guns on its shoulders." Castro says. "For this design, we had to fit the Milano's cockpit into a new spaceship, but keep the structure and building method of the Ravagers' spaceships."

CHAPTER SEVEN: KNOWHERE TO RUN

Roberto Fernández Castro concept art.

CHAPTER SEVEN: KNOWHERE TO RUN

Tim Hill concept art.

"The director wanted big shards that looked like dangerous broken glass on mechanical arms." Concept Artist Chris Rosewarne says of this new take on display screens. "This was passed on to some of our engineers who developed and made arms that could hold these big pieces of Plexiglas in position.

"What was really nice about doing the entire film was that the director and the designer said, 'That's been done, let's try something like this.'"

Chris Rosewarne concept art.

CHAPTER SEVEN: KNOWHERE TO RUN

YONDU UDONTA

"We thought it would be great to attach pieces of clothing from his conquests to his outfit," Concept Artist Rodney Fuentebella says. "I was happy that Michael Rooker was cast to play Yondu, as I used him as inspiration even before he was signed up."

Rodney Fuentebella concept art.

Justin Sweet concept art.

Jackson Sze concept art.

CHAPTER SEVEN: KNOWHERE TO RUN

"Yondu has a signature red fin/mohawk in the comics, and his trademark blue skin needed to be kept, as well," Concept Artist Jackson Sze says. "Here I was trying to go for a Yondu with a more elaborate braided beard and jewelries—exotic gems and rings he has collected from his pirating in space."

Jackson Sze concept art.

Rodney Fuentebella concept art.

Rodney Fuentebella concept art.

Justin Sweet concept art.

THE RAVAGERS

Howard Swindell/SMUFX concept art.

Howard Swindell/SMUFX concept art.

Concept art by Nigel Booth & Colin Shulver/SMUFX.

David White/SMUFX concept art.

CHAPTER SEVEN: KNOWHERE TO RUN

289

Costume Illustrator Warren Holder created early versions of cloaked Ravagers when Costume Designer Alexandra Byrne wanted to try alternate shapes. "The cloaks were intended to be worn over the flight suit," he says. "They were more an extension of the Ravagers characters, intended to convey an air of mystery."

Warren Holder concept art.

"There were different generations of Ravagers," Byrne says. "So we had about four different basic styles of clothing, going from a very backdated one to the most contemporary one." Meanwhile, Costume Illustrator Jack Dudman worked up a series of designs for the Guardians' flame symbol, again accounting for the various time periods.

Jack Dudman concept art.

CHAPTER SEVEN: KNOWHERE TO RUN

When the Guardians suit up in contemporary Ravager garb, they begin to resemble a team for the first time. "The burgundy-ochre colors are the Ravagers' common theme," Byrne says. "The Ravagers are all individuals, but they need to have a kind of a gang feel. Color was a tool we used to divine that."

Jack Dudman concept art.

Andy Park concept art.

Andy Park concept art.

Charlie Wen concept art.

CHAPTER SEVEN: KNOWHERE TO RUN

"Practically, I wanted to put them together to make sure the uniforms worked well together," Head of Development Charlie Wen says. When the Guardians don the matching Ravager uniforms, the team selflessly comes together to answer the call to adventure. "It was important to do a team shot with the Guardians wearing the Ravager uniforms because this is the first time from a story point that we actually see them becoming a team, less of themselves individually and more united together."

Charlie Wen keyframe.

CHAPTER SEVEN: KNOWHERE TO RUN

CHAPTER EIGHT
SOMEBODY'S GOTTA DO IT

Pete Thompson concept art.

Fate brought them together. Now, as thousands of Sakaaran fighters fill the skies over Xandar, the Guardians have the opportunity to do "something good."

"The big battle at the end happens in the atmosphere, so it's not a space battle," Visual Effects Supervisor Stephane Ceretti says. "It's really like a dogfight in the clouds."

To lend the spaceships an air of realism, the VFX team studied the surfaces of actual planes. "We looked at how they fly, how they're made, all the flaps they have—all these things," Ceretti says. "We also had some helicopter shoots in Singapore and different places to see how the buildings look from aerial views. There's a big part of Singapore close to the sea, and that was our inspiration for some of the buildings and cities we have at the end. We always try to look at real life, and then elaborate from there."

Concept Artist Pete Thompson's illustration depicts the Ravager fighters and the Milano exiting the Ecclector. "In the end, I came up with the Ravager ships being suspended vertically like bats hanging in a cave. I think it gave the shot a slightly sinister feel while also being very tech-driven in its appearance."

Concept Artist Jackson Sze imagined Ronan's Sakaaran fighters filling the sky like a deadly swarm of bugs as they descended from the Dark Aster. "To organize the aerial battle, the configuration was supposed to mimic a neuroimaging scan of Peter Quill's mom. The lump in the middle reminds Quill of the tumor that took her. It was an interesting challenge trying to design the formation to look like a brain scan, while still making some kind of sense of what was flying out of Ronan's massive ship."

Jackson Sze keyframe.

"Groot's new ability brings a sense of wonder to the film," Concept Artist Rodney Fuentebella says. "Groot is a character who is so different from other Marvel Cinematic Universe characters. Anything goes with him, and that idea is fun to play with. I like how this is a gentle moment where Groot's ability to light up the way brings them together."

Rodney Fuentebella keyframes.

CHAPTER EIGHT: SOMEBODY'S GOTTA DO IT

Andy Park keyframe.

Arriving on Xandar, the Sakaaran fighters "go full-on kamikaze," Concept Artist Andy Park says. "This is pretty much nearing the climax of the film, and the enemy is desperate to win no matter the costs. It shows their determination as well as their loyalty to Ronan—and ultimately, Thanos."

Jackson Sze keyframe.

Drax's rematch with Ronan does not unfold as he had imagined. "To portray Ronan's incredible power, he needed to absolutely dominate Drax," Sze says. "The fact that he can hold Drax up with one hand speaks to Ronan's strength. We debated about whether Ronan's body should be facing the audience or not. This one where he looks over his shoulder to see Rocket crashing through proved to be more interesting visually."

CHAPTER EIGHT: SOMEBODY'S GOTTA DO IT

"Groot grows out his branches, fills them with leaves, and then creates a cocoon to protect his friends from the fire," Concept Artist Anthony Francisco says. "This is one of the many memorable things Groot does in the movie. He is definitely a character the audience will enjoy."

Anthony Francisco keyframe.

CHAPTER EIGHT: SOMEBODY'S GOTTA DO IT

"Groot brings Rocket closer to him, his eyes saying goodbye, while Rocket's say 'you don't have to do this,'" Francisco says. "This had to have tremendous emotional impact, and that was at the back of my mind while I was painting this keyframe. I hope I was able to capture an endearing moment between best buds."

Anthony Francisco keyframe.

CHAPTER EIGHT: SOMEBODY'S GOTTA DO IT

"I wanted to make sure the crash felt like it was destroying a huge part of the city," Concept Artist Rodney Fuentebella says of the Dark Aster's descent to Xandar. "This was a great and fun film to work on. There is so much visual variety that painting all the different shapes and designs in this movie was never boring."

Rodney Fuentebella keyframe.

CHAPTER EIGHT: SOMEBODY'S GOTTA DO IT

Olivier Pron concept art.

CHAPTER EIGHT: SOMEBODY'S GOTTA DO IT

Andy Park keyframe.

CHAPTER EIGHT: SOMEBODY'S GOTTA DO IT

"This is the climax of the film where they are able to overcome impossible odds by working together—or in this case, literally holding each others' hands," Park says. "It's undoubtedly a powerful scene where they are all willing to make the ultimate sacrifice in one last desperate act.

"Working on the *Guardians of the Galaxy* film was definitely the most unique experience so far during my tenure here at Marvel Studios. It's a property that most people, myself included, were not very familiar with. It is—in a lot of ways—the most daring film for Marvel to tackle. But that is exactly why getting to work on it from the ground up was so gratifying. Because of its relative obscurity, we were open to really explore ideas and looks for these worlds and characters."

"Ronan is defeated and swept away by the enigmatic power of the Orb, made possible by the united power of the *Guardians of the Galaxy*," Park says. "It was a pleasure to paint this powerful climax to the movie. These misfits—or 'losers,' as Star-Lord calls them—are now one as a team."

Andy Park keyframe.

CHAPTER EIGHT: SOMEBODY'S GOTTA DO IT

Jackson Sze keyframe.

CHAPTER EIGHT: SOMEBODY'S GOTTA DO IT

"The first thing that really attracted me to *Guardians of the Galaxy* was creating a visually different type of space opera," Director and Co-Writer James Gunn says. "That meant taking the grit and dirt elements of the movies of the past 30 years or so, but also taking some of the bright colors of the beauty and the splendor of earlier space epics."

Fantastic But Grounded.
Originality Without Being Weird.
Bright Colors.
Grandosity.
Contrasts Are Good.

"We are not afraid to go over the top," Gunn wrote in 2012, in an initial document outlining his approach to the film's visuals. "No one will ever describe *Guardians of the Galaxy* as meek."

CHAPTER NINE
MARKETING GUARDIANS OF THE GALAXY

Star-Lord. Gamora. Drax. Rocket. Groot. Five little-known characters hooked the public imagination on a feeling during the months leading up to the release of Marvel's *Guardians of the Galaxy*.

"James wanted grit to the film, but he also wanted a vibrant look," Production Designer Charles Wood says. "He wanted something that was completely bold and colorful, where the design statements were strong. Both James and the studio wanted to pull away from the typical colorless world that we've seen a lot of in past science-fiction films."

And the first teaser poster reflected that. The sky behind the heroes matched the vibrant colors Gunn outlined in his 2012 document *Guardians of the Galaxy: The Visuals*. "Outer-space reds, blues, and purples—generally what I think of as 'Jim Starlin' colors—are central to our palette," Gunn wrote. In writer/artist and sometimes colorist Jim Starlin's comics, outer space had been dyed violet, ultramarine, cerulean, and carmine—a frontier of possibilities. Even as science-fiction films became starker and grittier through the decades, and coloring tools evolved from watercolors to markers to digital, Marvel's cosmos stuck with Starlin's space aesthetic, reflecting and celebrating the diversity and optimism of the unknown.

In addition to this sense of fun and wonder, the marketing for *Guardians of the Galaxy* needed to reflect the film's tongue-in-cheek feel while maintaining the action and excitement of the most colorful space odyssey in decades. Fans loved the simplicity of "You're Welcome," the first poster's tagline, and the cocky attitude mirrored in the trailers. This was a whole new kind of super-hero film.

First theatrical teaser poster.

Theatrical one-sheet.

CHAPTER NINE: MARKETING GUARDIANS OF THE GALAXY

Individual character posters.

CHAPTER NINE: MARKETING GUARDIANS OF THE GALAXY

Charlie Wen keyframe.

AFTERWORD

The Marvel Cinematic Universe was born in 2008 with the release of Marvel's *Iron Man* and *The Incredible Hulk*. Following that came a lineup that included *Iron Man 2*, *Thor*, *Captain America: The First Avenger*, *Marvel's The Avengers*, *Iron Man 3*, *Thor: The Dark World*, and *Captain America: The Winter Soldier*. All of these films are based on some of Marvel's most popular icons, and all more or less belong in the same world, sharing story lines and comic-book history. Then, President of Marvel Studios Kevin Feige announced that James Gunn was chosen to direct the *Guardians of the Galaxy*, which was the beginning of our development of Marvel's first expansion pack. With this expansion came new kinds of aliens, civilizations, and heroes—notably a walking tree and a talking raccoon, who both lived in a part of our universe that we had not yet seen. All of which would need to be researched and designed to live along with, and perhaps one day overlap, the world and lives of our other heroes. This was going to be exhilarating and challenging, and the Marvel Cinematic Universe would continue to evolve.

The main characters were no longer super heroes the likes of Thor and Captain America. Since this story was about the formation of the Guardians, there were two looks of the heroes that we focused on: the pre-team look and team-uniform look. Beyond our typical design challenges, much focus was put into designing Rocket and Groot. In fact, much of the success of this film would be conditioned upon a believable, compelling, and likable Rocket and Groot. We knew going into this that if the audience didn't buy these two heroes, the film would suffer—no matter how good the rest of it was. Rocket's kickoff began with the visitation of a raccoon to our offices in Manhattan Beach. We were able to study the mammal's movements, gestures, and other qualities that could be useful for our hero.

Although we generated a multitude of design directions, James was very clear early on that he wanted Rocket to undoubtedly be a raccoon, not just like one from an Earthly perspective. I believe we came up with endearing solutions for both Groot and Rocket, which can be partially seen in this book, but much of the amazing work will only be seen as they come to life for the first time on the big screen.

Creating the various characters, aliens, worlds, and technology of Guardians was on a scope Marvel had never seen in its previous films. Everything needed to be designed from scratch, and much needed to be built. Research was heavy and necessary to create characters, costumes, and keyframes that would each do their part in taking the audience on a believable space odyssey that is unique to Marvel. We had some incredible art, costumes, and prosthetics departments, led by Production Designer Charles Wood, Costume Designer Alexandra Byrne, and Special Make-up Effects Designer David White. My job was to lead Marvel's Visual Development team in designing the main heroes and villains, as well as developing the story keyframes that the director envisioned for the film. As with all of our films since *Iron Man*, Kevin Feige entrusted our VisDev team—which on this project consisted of Andy Park, Jackson Sze, Josh Herman, Rodney Fuentebella, Andrew Kim, Anthony Francisco, Justin Sweet, Jared Merantz, Kevin Chen, Iain McCaig, Jacob Johnston, and myself—to create a design aesthetic that would not only be cohesive with our MCU, but stand tall among generations of space epics.

Charlie Wen 2014

327

Director **James Gunn** began his filmmaking career with an eight-millimeter camera at the age of 12. His first film featured his brother Sean—later an actor on the WB's *The Gilmore Girls*—being disemboweled by zombies. While attending Columbia University, Gunn applied for a part-time job filing papers at famed B-movie studios Troma Entertainment and ended up writing the screenplay for the movie *Tromeo & Juliet* instead—for $150. In 1997, *Tromeo* became a cult hit. In 2000, Gunn wrote and starred in the *The Specials*, a film about a group of super heroes on their day off. In the same year, Bloomsbury Press released Gunn's critically acclaimed novel *The Toy Collector*. He also wrote, with Lloyd Kaufman, the nonfiction book *All I Need To Know About Filmmaking I Learned From The Toxic Avenger*. Gunn wrote the screenplay for the 2002 film *Scooby-Doo*, and in March of 2004, Gunn became the first screenwriter in cinema history to write back-to-back #1-for-the-weekend box office hits, with the critically acclaimed, re-imagined *Dawn of the Dead* and *Scooby-Doo: Monsters Unleashed*. Gunn's love for the comedy and horror genres coalesced in 2006's humorous horror film *Slither*. Gunn wrote the film, his feature-film directorial debut, which was named "The Best Horror film of 2006" by *Rue Morgue Magazine*, and Gunn won a Saturn Award and a Fangoria Chainsaw Award for his work on the film. In 2008, Gunn created Xbox Live's first original content, including his own *Sparky & Mikaela*. Also in 2008, Gunn hosted the reality show *Scream Queens* for VH1. Gunn most recently wrote and directed the independent feature film, *Super*, which was an official selection at the Toronto Film Festival, was picked up by IFC Films, and is IFC's top-selling film on On Demand. In 2012, Gunn released his first video game, *Lollipop Chainsaw*, with Suda 51 and Warner Bros. on Xbox and PlayStation 3.

Over the past decade, Producer and Marvel Studios President **Kevin Feige** has played an instrumental role in a string of blockbuster feature films adapted from the pages of Marvel comic books. In his current role, Feige oversees all creative aspects of the company's feature film and home entertainment activities. In addition to producing *Guardians of the Galaxy*, he is currently producing *Marvel's Avengers: Age of Ultron* and *Ant-Man*. His previous producing credits for Marvel include *Iron Man 3*, which became the second-largest box office debut in Hollywood history behind the critically acclaimed *Marvel's The Avengers*, which Kevin also produced along with *Captain America: The Winter Soldier*, *Thor: The Dark World*, *Thor*, *Captain America: The First Avenger*, *Iron Man 2* and *Iron Man*.

Executive Producer and Marvel Studios Co-President **Louis D'Esposito** served as Executive Producer on the blockbuster hits *Iron Man*, *Iron Man 2*, *Thor*, *Captain America: The First Avenger*, *Marvel's The Avengers*, *Iron Man 3*, *Thor: The Dark World* and most recently *Captain America: The Winter Soldier*. He is currently working on *Marvel's Avengers: Age of Ultron* and *Ant-Man*, as well as collaborating with Marvel Studios' President Kevin Feige to build the future Marvel slate. As co-president of the studio and executive producer on all Marvel films, D'Esposito balances running the studio to overseeing each film from its development stage to distribution. Beyond his role as co-president, D'Esposito also directs unique filmed projects for the studio, including his one-shot titled *Agent Carter* starring Hayley Atwell, and the short film titled *Item 47*. The project was released as an added feature on *Marvel's The Avengers* Blu-ray disc. D'Esposito began his tenure at Marvel Studios in 2006. Prior to Marvel, D'Esposito's executive producing credits include the 2006 hit film *The Pursuit of Happyness* starring Will Smith, *Zathura: A Space Adventure* and the 2003 hit *S.W.A.T.* starring Samuel L. Jackson and Colin Farrell.

Executive Producer **Victoria Alonso** is currently Executive Producer for writer/director Joss Whedon's *Avengers: Age of Ultron* for Marvel Studios, where she serves as Executive Vice President of Visual Effects and Post Production. She executive produced Joe and Anthony Russo's *Captain America: The Winter Soldier*, Alan Taylor's *Thor: The Dark World*, Shane Black's *Iron Man 3*, as well as *Marvel's The Avengers* for Joss Whedon. She also co-produced Marvel's *Iron Man* and *Iron Man 2* with Director Jon Favreau, Kenneth Branagh's *Thor* and Joe Johnston's *Captain America: The First Avenger*. Alonso's career began at the nascency of the visual effects industry, when she served as a commercial VFX producer. From there, she VFX-produced numerous feature films, working with such directors as Ridley Scott (*Kingdom of Heaven*), Tim Burton (*Big Fish*) and Andrew Adamson (*Shrek*), to name a few.

Anthony Francisco concept art.

CONTRIBUTOR BIOS 2014

Executive Producer **Jeremy Latcham** is the senior vice president of production and development at Marvel Studios, where he served as an executive producer on the 2012 blockbuster hit *Marvel's The Avengers*, which shattered box office records. Latcham is currently working as an Executive Producer alongside writer/director Joss Whedon on *Marvel's Avengers: Age of Ultron*, the sequel to *Marvel's The Avengers*. Latcham served as Associate Producer on the 2008 critically acclaimed blockbuster *Iron Man* and as co-producer on the hit 2010 follow-up *Iron Man 2*. A graduate of Northwestern University, Latcham began his career at Miramax and Dimension Films and also worked at the Endeavor Agency. In 2004, he joined Marvel Studios where he has also held the titles of vice president, director of development, and creative executive. In 2011, Latcham was featured as one of "Hollywood's New Leaders" by *Variety*.

Executive Producer **Nikolas Korda** lists co-producer on Ridley Scott's *Robin Hood* and Chris Weitz's *The Golden Compass* amongst his credits. As a Unit Production Manager, Korda's credits include most recently Ridley Scott's *Prometheus* (as well as *Robin Hood*), Jonathan Liebesman's *Wrath of the Titans*, Tim Burton's *Charlie and the Chocolate Factory*, Peter Jackson's *Lord of the Rings* trilogy and Stephen Hopkins' *Lost In Space*. He has also worked as an assistant director on several films including Tim Burton's *Batman*, Richard Attenborough's *Cry Freedom*, Jim Henson's *Labyrinth*, as well as *Rambo III* and *Hamburger Hill*. He is currently executive producer on *Tarzan* for Warner Brothers.

Co-Producer **David J. Grant** started with Marvel Studios in 2008 as vice president of Physical Production. David oversaw production on *Iron Man 2*, *Thor*, *Marvel's The Avengers* (also associate producer), *Thor: The Dark World* (also associate producer) and *Guardians of the Galaxy*. Current projects include *Ant-Man* and *Dr. Strange*. Prior to directly joining Marvel Studios, David was a freelance production supervisor having most recently supervised *Fast and Furious*, *Iron Man*, *Spider-Man 3* and *Spider-Man 2*. He also worked for 20 years with industry veteran Executive Producer Joseph Caracciolo Sr., first as his personal assistant and then as production supervisor.

Co-Producer and Vice President of Production and Development **Jonathan Schwartz** began his career at Marvel Studios in 2008. Schwartz served as Kevin Feige's assistant on *Iron Man 2*, *Thor*, and *Captain America: The First Avenger*, and as Creative Executive on *Marvel's The Avengers*. *Guardians of the Galaxy* is the first feature film that he has overseen for the studio. An alumnus of Pomona College, Schwartz previously worked at the William Morris Agency.

Production Designer **Charles Wood** began his entertainment-industry career in 1991 as a visual effects art director on such projects as *The Fugitive*, Peter Weir's *Fearless*, *Under Siege* and Sam Raimi's *Army of Darkness*. Segueing to design work, he has since collaborated on projects ranging from big studio movies to independent films. Wood is currently working on Joss Whedon's *Marvel's Avengers: Age of Ultron*. His credits include James Gunn's *Guardians of the Galaxy*, *Thor: The Dark World*, Joe Carnahan's *The A-Team*, Michael Apted's *Amazing Grace*, *Wrath of the Titans*, *Fool's Gold*, Tony Bill's *Flyboys*, F. Gary Gray's *The Italian Job*, *Get Carter* and *Mortal Kombat: Annihilation*. Wood earned an Emmy Award nomination in 2000 for the TV movie *Geppetto* and a 2007 Satellite Award nomination for *Amazing Grace*.

Costume Designer **Alexandra Byrne** trained as an architect at Bristol University before studying Theatre Design on the Motley Course at the English National Opera under the legendary Margaret Harris. She has worked extensively in television and theater, both as a set and costume designer. Her television credits include Roger Michell's *Persuasion*, for which she received the BAFTA Award for Best Costume Design, and *The Buddha of Suburbia*, for which she received a BAFTA nomination and RTS award. In theater, Byrne received a Tony nomination for Best Set Design for *Some Americans Abroad*, which transferred from the Royal Shakespeare Company to the Lincoln Center in New York. Following her work in theater, Byrne designed the costumes for Kenneth Branagh's *Hamlet*, for which she gained her first Oscar nomination. Other credits include *Phantom of the Opera*, *Sleuth* and *The Garden of Eden*. She received two further Oscar nominations for her costumes in Elizabeth and *Finding Neverland*. Elizabeth, *The Golden Age* finally won her the Oscar. Byrne worked with Kenneth Branagh again on *Thor*, her first production with Marvel, and won the Saturn Award. She then worked with Joss Whedon on *Marvel's The Avengers*. After designing costumes for Warner's *300, Rise of an Empire*, Byrne returned to Marvel for James Gunn's *Guardians of the Galaxy* and is currently working with Joss Whedon again on Marvel's *Avengers: Age of Ultron*. Byrne is married to the actor Simon Shepherd, and they have four children.

Director of Photography **Ben Davis**'s feature film credits include Jonathan Liebesman's *Wrath of the Titans*, John Madden's *The Best Exotic Marigold Hotel* and *The Debt*, Mikael Håfström's *The Rite*, Stephen Frears' *Tamara Drewe*, Gerald McMorrow's *Franklyn*, Sharon Maguire's *Incendiary* and Peter Webber's *Hannibal Rising*. Davis has collaborated extensively with director Matthew Vaughn on *Layer Cake*, *Stardust*, and *Kick-Ass*. Davis' work can also be seen in the short film, *The Tonto Woman*, which received an Academy Award® nomination in 2008 for Best Live Action short film. Davis' recent credits include Martin McDonagh's *Seven Psychopaths*, starring Sam Rockwell, Christopher Walken, Woody Harrelson and Colin Farrell; Dan Mazer's *I Give It A Year*; Pascal Chaumeil's *A Long Way Down*; and Rowan Joffe's *Before I Go To Sleep*, starring Nicole Kidman and Colin Firth.

Head of Visual Development **Charlie Wen** has held a variety of positions in the entertainment industry, ranging from concept designer to art director, on everything from feature films to video games and animation. Wen's client list reads as a virtual who's who of the industry, including Disney, Digital Domain, Dreamworks, Legendary Pictures, Marvel Studios, Darkhorse, Rhythm and Hues, Imagi Studios, Wizards of the Coast, and Sony Computer Entertainment of America. In 2005, he created Kratos and helped establish *God of War* as a monolithic action-adventure title for Sony PlayStation. Outside the production environment, Wen has given lectures on figure drawing and character design at many distinguished studios and universities. After helping establish the main character designs in *Thor*, he holds the title of head of visual development at Marvel Studios, working on Marvel's *Captain America: The First Avenger*, *Marvel's The Avengers*, *Iron Man 3*, *Thor: The Dark World*, *Guardians of the Galaxy*, *Captain America: The Winter Soldier*, *Marvel's Avengers: Age of Ultron* and *Ant-Man*.

Special Makeup Effects/Prosthetics Designer **David White** began his career at age 19 as an assistant to Makeup Effects Artist Nick Maley on *The Keep* (1982). White went to work for Creature Effects Designer Lyle Conway on *Return to Oz* (1983) as a sculptor, and again for Maley on *Lifeforce* (1984). White joined the makeup effects team on *Little Shop of Horrors* (1985) as senior painter and animatronics technician of the Audrey II plants. Following his work on Mary Shelley's *Frankenstein* (1994) as a makeup effects designer, White formed his own company, Altered States FX, with business partner Sacha Carter. Based at Shepperton Studios, White oversaw all prosthetic work from design to final on-set application on many projects. He received his first Emmy Award nomination for the TNT movie *The Hunchback*; his prosthetic design work on Robbie Williams in the music video for "Rock DJ" became a multi-award winner in the Best Special Effects category. He worked on Ridley Scott's *Kingdom of Heaven* and Tony Scott's *Spy Game*, also creating prosthetics for films such as *The Da Vinci Code*, *La Vie en Rose*, and *Bruges*. He subsequently served as head of department on films such as Ridley Scott's *Robin Hood*, Joe Johnston's *Captain America: The First Avenger* and *Snow White and the Huntsman*. Prior to heading up Special Makeup Effects for *Guardians of the Galaxy*, his most recent credits as special makeup designer include Disney's *Maleficent* and Marvel's *Thor: The Dark World*.

Property Master **Barry Gibbs** has worked in film since 1981, when he started his career as a stagehand with model units on *Krull* and *Supergirl*, with The Rank Organisation at Pinewood Studios. He shortly moved to props, where his first jobs included Ridley Scott's *Legend* and the Bond film *A View To A Kill*. Gibbs gained experience in the disciplines of set dressing and standing by on set, then went freelance in 1985 with Julien Temple's *Absolute Beginners*. Three years later, he had the first offer of a prop master position on Roald Dahl's *Danny the Champion of the World*. At that time, he split his efforts between feature films and commercials. This continued until 1993, when Gibbs went to Ireland for *Circle of Friends* with Production Designer Jim Clay. Since then, he has worked on *Captain Corelli's Mandolin*, *About a Boy*, *Love Actually*, *Timeline*, *The Golden Compass*, *Quantum of Solace* and *Inception*, among others. Gibbs' avid interest in manufacturing keeps him involved with and running large prop shops with amazing teams of technicians. He was given the opportunity to work for Marvel on *Captain America: The First Avenger*, *Thor: The Dark World*, *Guardians of the Galaxy*, and is currently working on *Marvel's Avengers: Age of Ultron*.

Visual Effects Supervisor **Stephane Ceretti** is a native of France, with a background in physics and the arts. Ceretti started in the VFX industry working as a digital artist for Buf Compagnie in Paris in 1996. He began his career with *Batman and Robin* and then moved to numerous commercials where he acquired all the skills to supervise both shoot and post, before advancing to VFX supervisor for Buf on Tarsem's *The Cell*. From this point, Ceretti has been involved as VFX supervisor on major feature films such as the Wachowskis' *Matrix* sequels, as well as Oliver Stone's *Alexander*. In the last few years, Ceretti sharpened his supervisor skills on various genres of films from *Harry Potter 4* to *Batman Begins* and *Silent Hill*. Ceretti has been overall VFX supervisor for his last two projects at Buf: *The Prestige* by world-acclaimed Director Christopher Nolan, as well as the latest movie from French Director Mathieu Kassovitz, *Babylon AD*, a Fox/Studio Canal production. He then joined MPC and Method studios in London where he supervised the VFX work on movies like *Prince of Persia: The Sands of Time*. Ceretti's first adventure with Marvel Studios was to be the 2nd VFX supervisor on the shoot of Joe Johnston's *Captain America: The First Avenger*. After joining Fox Studios to work with John Dykstra as an additional VFX supervisor on Matthew Vaughn's *X-Men: First Class*, he co-supervised with Dan Glass the Visual Effects of the Warner Bros. movie *Cloud Atlas* directed by Lana and Andy Wachowski and Tom Tykwer. Following his work on *Thor: The Dark World* as a 2nd Unit Supervisor, he joined Marvel's *Guardians of the Galaxy* as the main VFX supervisor.

Visual Effects Producer **Susan Pickett** began her career in film as a production assistant in New York, where she worked as a set PA and a 2nd AD on numerous features before transitioning into VFX. She worked as a VFX coordinator on several films involving VFX and animation—including *Fat Albert*, *Garfield: A Tale of Two Kitties* and *Fantastic Four: Rise of the Silver Surfer*. She then linked up with Marvel's Executive Producer Victoria Alonso, and worked as VFX production manager on *Iron Man*. Now working as a VFX producer, she has been at Marvel for eight years and has worked on *Iron Man 2*, *Marvel's The Avengers* in addition to *Guardians of the Galaxy*. In addition to working on over 30 feature films, Susan is both a member of the Director's Guild of America and the Producer's Guild of America.

Concept Artist **Andy Park** began his career illustrating comic books on titles such as *Tomb Raider*, *Excalibur* and *Uncanny X-Men* for companies like Marvel, DC and Image Comics. In 2004, he began working as a concept artist in video games and television. He was one of the leading artists creating the worlds and characters of the award-winning *God of War* franchise for Sony Computer Entertainment of America. Park has since joined the team at Marvel Studios as a visual development illustrator, designing characters and keyframes for *Marvel's The Avengers*, *Captain America: The First Avenger*, *Iron Man 3*, *Captain America: The Winter Soldier*, *Thor: The Dark World* and the upcoming *Avengers: Age of Ultron*.

Concept Artist **Jackson Sze** has worked in advertising, video games, television and film for studios such as Lucasfilm Animation and Sony Computer Entertainment of America. He is a founding member of the BATTLEMiLK series of art books and is a Senior Concept Illustrator at Marvel Studios. His projects include *Marvel's The Avengers*, *Thor: The Dark World* and *Avengers: Age of Ultron*.

Concept Artist **Anthony Francisco** worked on film and game projects before moving into movie concept art for various effects houses such as Stan Winston Studios, Rick Baker, ADI, Harlow FX and Illusion Industries. Francisco produced art for *Superman Returns*, *A.I. Artificial Intelligence*, *Men in Black 2*, *Spider-Man*, *The Passion of the Christ*, *G.I Joe: Retaliation* and *The Chronicles of Riddick*, among others. From 2004-2006, he worked as a concept artist at NCsoft Santa Monica on the *Guild Wars* and *Tabula Rasa* MMO game titles. Anthony then joined the team at Offset Software as lead concept artist to work on a fantasy-based FPS game. In 2010, he worked at Rhythm and Hues on *Hunger Games*, *RIPD* and *Seventh Son*. Anthony also does illustration work for *Magic: The Gathering* and has been an instructor at Gnomon School for Visual Effects, Art Center College of Design in Pasadena, Concept Design Academy and CGMW online. He is based in Burbank where he works on upcoming Marvel titles as part of the Visual Development team at Marvel Studios.

Storyboard Artist **David Krentz** was born in Winnipeg, Canada, and graduated from the Character Animation program at California Institute of the Arts in 1993. He was immediately hired into Walt Disney Feature Animation as a layout artist. He migrated into a lead character designer position for a four-year long stint on Disney's *Dinosaur*. His love for dinosaurs, anatomy and character proved a valuable asset to that benchmark CG film. After leaving Disney he went on to pursue a freelance career, where he stretched his creative wings doing many different kinds of jobs on many different projects including sculpting (digital and clay), storyboarding, creature/character design and concept illustration. He contributed to such movies as *Fantasia 2000*, *Dinosaur*, *Treasure Planet*, *Spider-Man 2*, *Valiant*, *The Ant Bully*, *Outlander*, *The Spiderwick Chronicles*, the *Walking With Dinosaurs* 3-D feature, *John Carter* and *Ant-Man*. He took on the role of director for the Discovery Channel series *Dinosaur Revolution* as well as the CG animated feature film *Dinotasia* with Werner Herzog. He maintains ties to the scientific community, where he often lectures on developing performance-centric creatures for film and recreates new dinosaur finds from the bones up. He also stars in a "how to draw dinosaurs" series of DVDs and has become one of the most respected figures in the world of dinosaur art.

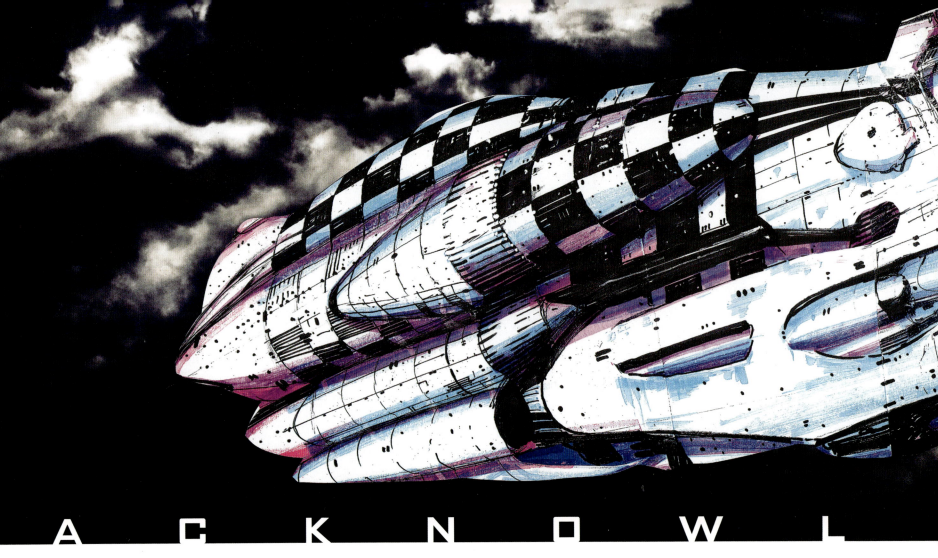

ACKNOWL

Dan Abnett	Bob Cheshire	Alan Fine	Simon Hatt
Victoria Alonso	Graham Churchyard	Luke Fisher	Josh Herman
Ron Ashtiani	Stephane Ceretti	Framestore	Greg Hildebrandt
Atomhawk Design	Glenn Close	Anthony Francisco	Tim Hildebrandt
Dave Bautista	Gabriele Dell'otto	Rodney Fuentebella	Tim Hill
John Beatty	Louis D'Esposito	Alexander Gaeta	Warren Holder
Nigel Booth	Romek Delimata	Keith Giffen	Djimon Hounsou
Alexandra Byrne	Benicio Del Toro	Karen Gillan	Fliss Jaine
Christopher Caldow	Juan Doe	Adi Granov	Kevin Jenkins
Joe Caramagna	Colleen Doran	David J. Grant	Jacob Johnston
Roberto Fernández Castro	Jack Dudman	Tim Green II	Nikolas Korda
Paul Catling	Nathan Fairbairn	James Gunn	Melia Kreiling
Kevin Chen	Kevin Feige	Guru-eFX	Magdalena Kusowska

Chris Foss concept art.

ACKNOWLEDGMENTS

Theodore W. Kutt
Clint Langley
Andy Lanning
Jeremy Latcham
Stan Lee
Ron Lim
Rick Magyar
Jerad Marantz
Stephan Martinière
Iain McCaig
Ryan Meinerding
Steve Montano
Method Studios

Moving Picture Co.
Lee Pace
Andy Park
Alan Payne
Paul Pelletier
Chris Pratt
Olivier Pron
John C. Reilly
Michael Rooker
Bill Rosemann
Chris Rosewarne
Eleni Roussos
Zoe Saldana

Andy Schmidt
Jonathan Schwartz
Colin Shulver
Jim Starlin
Evelyn Stein
Aaron Steven
Justin Sweet
Howard Swindell
Jackson Sze
Pete Thompson
Victoria Tracconi
Jim Valentino
Oliver Van Der Vijver

Tom Vincent
Dan Walker
Charlie Wen
David White
Charles Wood
Loïc e338 Zimmermann

ARTISTS CREDITS

Charlie Wen
Pages 2-3; 6-7; 18-19; 22; 24; 52; 90-92; 98-99; 116-117; 118; 122; 130; 133; 137; 140-143; 160-161; 162; 166-167; 185; 199; 270-273; 293-295; 326-327

Andy Park
Pages 4-5; 20-21; 23; 91; 102-105; 107; 110-111; 132; 135-137; 138-139; 144-145; 161; 165; 197-198; 200; 260-261; 262-263; 292-293; 302-303; 314-317

Chris Foss
Pages 8; 332-333

Tim Hill
Pages 16-17; 74-75; 77; 83-85; 182; 274-275; 280-281

Kevin Chen
Page 21

Josh Herman
Pages 24; 126; 128; 184-185

Rodney Fuentebella
Pages 25; 190-191; 239; 284; 286-287; 300-301; 310-311

Chris Rosewarne
Pages 26-28; 35; 64; 68-69; 86-87; 282-283

Moving Picture Co.
Pages 29; 120-121; 125

Kevin Jenkins
Pages 30-31; 33; 232-233; 255

Justin Sweet
Pages 32-33; 40-41; 50; 93-95; 106; 123; 163-164; 192-193; 196-197; 199; 201-203; 238; 285; 287

Bob Cheshire
Pages 34-35; 36-37; 38; 78-81

Oliver Van Der Vijver
Page 38

Jack Dudman
Pages 42; 89; 113-114; 134; 158-159; 184; 206; 240; 242-244; 291-292; Gatefold

Jackson Sze
Pages 43; 44; 48; 106; 112-113; 115; 124; 129; 132; 136; 146-147; 163; 165; 167; 216-217; 234-235; 256; 285-286; 298-299; 304-305; 318-319

Anthony Francisco
Pages 45; 49; 51; 79; 115; 131; 164; 185; 188-189; 238-239; 249; 259; 260-261; 261; 306-309; 328-329

Jerad Marantz
Pages 46-47; 185

Christopher Caldow
Pages 53; 207-209

Roberto Fernández Castro
Pages 54-63; 154-157; 246-247; 250-254; 276-2797; Gatefold

Paul Catling
Pages 61; 70-73; 76; 82; 88-89; 113; 168-171; 210-211

Dan Walker
Pages 63; 93

Romek Delimata
Pages 64-67

Pete Thompson
Pages 76; 174-181; 183; 186-187; 233; 236-237; 266-267; 276-277; 296-297

David White & Special Make-Up Effects
Pages 89; 112; 184; 289

Loïc e338 Zimmermann
Pages 96-97

Olivier Pron
Pages 108-109; 148-153; 312-313

Warren Holder
Pages 113; 240; 290

Nigel Booth
Pages 112; 289

Colin Shulver
Pages 112; 184; 289

Luke Fisher
Page 112

Howard Swindell
Pages 112; 288

Ryan Meinerding
Pages 117; 185

Iain McCaig
Page 119

Phil Saunders
Pages 172-173

Stephan Martinière
Pages 182; 267

David Krentz
Pages 212-215; 218-229

Framestore
Pages 230-231

Magdalena Kusowska
Pages 241-245; 260

Andrew Kim
Pages 248-249

Richard Anderson
Pages 254-255

Gregory Fangeaux
Pages 266; 268-269